The Royalty
of
Negro Vaudeville

The Royalty

of

Negro Vaudeville

The Whitman Sisters *and*
the Negotiation *of* Race, Gender *and* Class
in African American Theater, 1900–1940

Nadine George-Graves

St. Martin's Press
New York

ISBN 0-312-22562-8

Library of Congress Cataloging-in-Publishing Data
George, Nadine.
  The royalty of Negro vaudeville : the Whitman Sisters and the negotiation of race, gender and class in African American theatre, 1900-1940 / by Nadine George.
      p. cm.
  ISBN 0-312-22562-8
      1. Whitman Sisters (Dance group) 2. Afro-American dancers—Biography. 3. Women dancers—United States—Biography. 4. Vaudeville—Social aspects. I. Title.

GV1785.A1 G46 2000
792.7'092'396073—dc21
[B]
                                                                                99-088103

Design by Acme Art, Inc.

First edition: July, 2000
10 9 8 7 6 5 4 3 2 1

Dedicated
to the memory of my mother,
Lorna George

Contents

Acknowledgments

I could not have completed this book without the generous assistance of many. First, thanks to the librarians and archivists who helped me locate the primary and secondary resources, without which there would have been no book. I am grateful to the many scholars who have been mentors and models of academic and artistic excellence and have kindly extended encouragement to me, particularly Jean-Claude Baker, Hazel Carby, Cathy Cohen, Cathy Cole, Rives Collins, Dwight Conquergood, Tracy Davis, Leslie Delmenico, Lynn Dierks, Brenda Dixon Gottschild, Margaret Thompson Drewel, Frank Galati, Paul Gilroy, Kim Holton, Emily Kelly, David Krasner, Robin Lakes, Susan Lee, Susan Manning, Heather McClure, Marisa Nordstom, Debbie Paredez, Diana Paulin, Mary Poole, Tim Raphael, Sandra L. Richards, Joseph Roach, Robert Stepto, William Worthen, and Mary Zimmerman. Thanks to Deborah Kirtman and Ernestine Lucas for sharing biographical information about the Whitman Sisters and personal anecdotes about family lore. The Hilles and Griswold funds provided me resources to help finish the manuscript. I would also like to thank Michael Flamini, Senior Editor of St. Martin's Scholarly and Reference Division, and the staff of St. Martin's Press. My aunt Ruby Rowe is a constant source of light and beauty, always reminding me of the truly important things in life. I owe my greatest debt to my husband, Cebra Graves, who has faithfully read and edited every iteration of this book and has been my rock throughout the process. Finally, this book is dedicated to the memory of my mother, Lorna George, the strongest woman I've ever known. May I live my life with a fraction of her power.

Preface

Surviving the Silence

We are deeply, passionately connected to black women whose sense of aesthetics, whose commitment to ongoing creative work, inspires and sustains. We reclaim their history, call their names, state their particulars, to gather and remember, to share our inheritance.

—bell hooks

[T]o survive in the mouth of this dragon we call America, we have had to learn this first and most vital lesson—that we were never meant to survive. Not as human beings. And that visibility which makes us most vulnerable is that which also is the source of our greatest strength. Because the machine will try to grind you into dust anyway, whether or not we speak.

—Audre Lorde

I FIRST CAME ACROSS JEAN STEARNS AND MARSHALL STEARNS' BOOK *Jazz Dance* while preparing a review of the literature on black dance during my first year in graduate school. Chapter 12 of this 45-chapter text on the dance greats of the jazz era is devoted entirely to the Whitman Sisters, a fascinating and extremely successful black vaudeville troupe. The Whitman Sisters, I learned, was the highest paid act on the Theatre Owners Booking Association (a.k.a. TOBA or Toby) circuit and one of the longest surviving touring companies. The troupe frequently changed its repertory with the times to assure that its performances remained popular. The Whitman Sisters was considered "the greatest incubator of dancing talent for Negro shows on or off T.O.B.A.,"[1] helping to foster the careers of tap dance greats Bill "Bojangles" Robinson, Jeni LeGon, and Pops and Louis; singer Ethel Waters; musician Count Basie; comedians Butterbeans and Susie; and many more. As I continued researching, finding smaller blurbs about the sisters in other dance and theater texts, I discovered that the Whitman sisters were remarkable both on and off stage. They fought for desegregation in theaters, stayed committed to African American communities, and promoted what I will argue were black feminist agendas.

I've loved dance and theater all my life and developed in college a feminist interest in exceptional black women. So why hadn't I heard of these four women? I spoke with other theater scholars and found only a few who knew of the sisters. Black theater and dance scholars and black cultural librarians were aware of the sisters, but even they could not tell me the details of their work or point to a definitive, extensive resource. The librarian at the Schomburg Center for Research in Black Culture remarked on how famous the Whitman Sisters were, but told me that she had no idea where to find further information on them. The Library of Congress also had no information on the Whitman Sisters. The collections did contain a few scripts for comedian Bert Williams and the troupe Black Patti's Troubadours, but by no means did the collections contain a sufficient number of sources on early African American theater for an extensive study. University collections, including those at Howard, Harvard, and Yale, were similarly lacking in source material. I was shocked by the scant resources but determined to find out as much as I could about these women. The more I investigated, the more I began to understand an all-too-common situation regarding African American performers of the Whitman Sisters' era. In many cases, scholars of this subject must do more investigative work than is necessary for other topics in order to locate resource materials. It may not be surprising to some to learn that many records regarding the Whitman Sisters, like those of so many other early black artists, have been lost or have not been archived or cross-referenced, and research facilities devoted to this type of material are generally understaffed and underfunded. The Schomburg Center is a notable exception, having a uniquely good collection of resources on African American arts and culture. Yet, it too has a very limited amount of information on the Whitman Sisters. As a result, the Whitman Sisters, like many other black acts of that era, has been largely forgotten or hidden from history.

❖ ❖ ❖

Two words keep echoing as I contemplate this work: silence and survival. How do I survive studying a history that has silenced so many of my foremothers and threatens to silence me? How can the Whitman sisters survive the institutionalized silencing that has almost erased them from national memory and nearly deleted them from history? How do we black women survive the silencing to which we have been subjected for centuries and combat the silencing and warping of images of ourselves?

Silencing works in many ways. The most obvious example pertinent to this work is the silencing of slaves in the antebellum South by white men. Black women were also silenced by white women during the women's suffrage movement of the 1900s and 1910s. Rosalyn Terborg-Penn reminds us that black women had to battle not only institutionalized disenfranchisement but also attempts from white women to exclude them from their dream. "Unfortunately, with little influence among white women, the black suffragists were powerless and their words went unheeded."[2]

Also, white feminist theorists often neglect to consider race and class as modes of oppression that complicate gender oppression or to recognize that the issues important to women of color may be different from those important to white women. As Evelyn Brooks Higginbotham tells us, "[W]hite feminist scholars pay hardly more than lip service to race as they continue to analyze their own experience in ever more sophisticated forms."[3] This failure to include race results in an absence of black women from feminists' literature and a silencing of black women from their discourse.

Black women were also silenced by black men during the 1960s black liberation movement as they were told to take a step back and let men lead the way. Paula Giddings explains that in periods of racial assertion throughout history and especially during the 1960s movement, black women tended to be "muted."[4] In her autobiography, Angela Davis discusses the ways in which she was silenced and asked to take a less active role in the movement. She says:

> I ran headlong into a situation which was to become a constant problem in my political life. I was criticized very heavily, especially by male members of [Ron] Karenga's organization, for doing a "man's job." Women should not play leadership roles, they insisted. A woman was to "inspire" her man and educate his children.[5]

The joke below, told by white male minstrels at the beginning of the twentieth century in blackface about black women, who of course were forbidden to share the stage with them, shows how the black female voice was something to be feared and suppressed. This example also illustrates the proliferation of silencing as part of American cultural production. Though performed in jest, the banter suggests that hers is a voice not to be heard.

> INTERLOCUTOR—I would like my wife to resemble a town clock . . . Because then she would speak but once an hour.
>
> BONES—Well, I wouldn't want my wife to resemble no town clock, for when she did speak, the whole town would hear her. . . . I couldn't stand that.
>
> INTERLOCUTOR—That is so. Well, I guess I would like my wife to resemble an echo.
>
> Bones—Why so?
>
> INTERLOCUTOR—Why then she would speak only when spoken to.
>
> BONES—No, sir. I wouldn't want my wife to resemble no echo.
>
> INTERLOCUTOR—Why not, Bones?
>
> BONES—Why, she'd always have the last word and that would break me all up.[6]

These are just a few examples of the proliferation of the silencing of African American women throughout history. But what are the results of this systematic silencing? Glenda Dickerson explains the damage done by silencing black women:

> That voice [of women of color] has been silenced for centuries, breaking forth sporadically, choked, and gasping for air. . . . The depiction and perception of African-American woman in this country through stereotypes has [sic] garbled her voice and distorted her image. The real tragedy is that the African-American woman herself has too frequently bought that distortion.[7]

So, we are presented with distorted images of African American women against which we find it difficult or impossible to speak. Part of my reasons for doing this work and writing this book is to provide accounts of black women that are true and not based on stereotypes so that history more accurately reflects the complexities of black female identity. I hope to make it more difficult to buy into the stereotypes by offering historical figures as examples.

Many black feminists and womanists have interrogated the ways in which black women have been silenced throughout history and have proposed strategies for breaking the silences and speaking about our concerns. Hazel Carby reminds us that historically, in order to gain public voice, black women have had to "confront the dominant domestic ideologies and literary conventions of womanhood which excluded them from the definition 'woman.'"[8] In an 1831 speech, Maria Stewart stated: "O, ye daughters of Africa, awake! awake! arise! no longer sleep nor slumber, but distinguish yourselves."[9] Audre Lorde also writes on the transformation of silence into language and action, arguing that black women have been rendered invisible by being silenced, and must speak in order to reclaim the language that has been made to work against us:

> We can learn to work and speak when we are afraid in the same way we have learned to work and speak when we are tired . . . and while we wait in silence for that final luxury of fearlessness, the weight of that silence will choke us.[10]

The challenge for many of us is to be able to speak using the full range of our voices, to attempt to express the totality of ourselves. And for black female scholars, that act of speaking out serves to locate our experiences within an intellectual framework and validate our histories. Talking back is tantamount to confronting those silencing hegemonic forces and to speaking as a peer, standing on equal ground with those in power. As bell hooks reminds us:

> Moving from silence into speech is for the oppressed, the colonized, the exploited, and those who stand and struggle side by side, a gesture of defiance that heals, that makes new life and new growth possible. It is that act of speech, of talking back, that is no mere gesture of empty words, that is the expression of our movement from object to subject— the liberated voice.[11]

As black women in the United States have been silenced, we have also been redefined, primarily by the white male hegemony that controls the systems dominating our lives. For black female performers, this system of silence and redefinition operates in terms of the roles we are permitted to play, the compensation we can expect to receive, and the criticism to which we are subjected. I argue that the Whitman sisters confronted these obstacles by challenging stereotypical roles, fighting for the salaries they deserved and pleasing many types of audiences and critics, garnering in the process exceptional reviews. They retained agency over their identities instead of accepting the labels imposed on them by others by speaking out for themselves in the press and in speeches before each show, explaining who they were and what their beliefs were. In this way, they resisted dominant forces and survived. By taking stands for their rights, by challenging expectations of what black women were "supposed" to do, and by owning and operating their company, the sisters survived in an industry not designed for them. As we look back on their lives, we see that as black women in the entertainment industry they made conscious efforts to assure their success. In this book I analyze how they were able to hold onto their images and define their identities despite opposition.

Although we black women were never meant to survive, we have done so, to much surprise and perhaps disappointment. Maya Angelou articulates the politics of oppression and the fact of our survival:

> The Black female is assaulted in her tender years by all those common forces of nature at the same time that she is caught in the tripartite crossfire of masculine prejudice, white illogical hate and Black lack of power.
>
> The fact that the adult American Negro female emerges a formidable character is often met with amazement, distaste and even belligerence. It is seldom accepted as an inevitable outcome of the struggle won by survivors and deserves respect if not enthusiastic acceptance.[12]

Silence immobilizes us, and there are so many silences to be broken. One important way to break the silences of history is to tell our stories, the stories of our foremothers and the stories that inspire us. In this book I attempt to tell the stories of these four women by analyzing the social and political forces in which (and more often against which) they operated. In this way, as we embark on the new millennium, we can learn from their stories and be inspired by their strengths.

But how can the Whitman sisters break through the silences of history, when they are so long dead? How can their narratives survive? How can their stories serve scholarship? How can we learn from their experiences? This is "when and where I enter."[13] In this book, I function as an archeologist in the tradition of VèVè Clark, attempting to break the silences by excavating the materials that have been buried and presumed lost in order to fill in the gaps and tell the stories of those forgotten.[14] Valuing all of the artifacts of history—textual, visual and oral—I compile the facts to describe and analyze their lives.

During this elaborate, historical treasure hunt I have evoked the Whitman sisters' ancestral spirits and have asked them to help me find what I need to tell their stories. Throughout this process, while paging through archives of black newspapers, some days finding only a nugget in terms of a line written about them, some days finding a gold mine of information that lent insight into some crucial outstanding question, and while organizing, assembling, analyzing, and writing about what I have discovered, I have felt the sisters' presence. I can fully appreciate now Alice Walker's spiritual journey to literally and metaphorically break the silence surrounding Zora Neale Hurston's life and career and to give her her deserved place in history.[15] Walker researched Hurston's work, persisted in finding her grave and putting a marker on it, and told the world of Hurston's literary importance. The more I have researched the Whitman sisters, the clearer it has become that like Hurston, the Whitman sisters deserve to, need to, and must be written back into history with the prominence that is rightfully theirs. Dancer Louis Williams told Jean and Marshall Stearns that "The Whitman sisters stood for something. They were the ones I was going to build a monument for on Broadway—they knew talent when they saw it and gave hundreds of dancers their first big break."[16] Though not a Broadway monument, it is my hope that this book serves as a tribute to their importance.

On a research trip to Atlanta I found the Whitman family plot in the Southview Cemetery. I was shocked and saddened by the lack of upkeep at the gravesite. I had to pull the weeds away to find Alberta Whitman's headstone, which was broken. Essie Whitman's headstone is all but buried by a wall erected after her death. Mabel Whitman's headstone is missing. Alice was buried in Lincoln Cemetery, North Township, Illinois. Nowhere at Southview is there any indication of the family's accomplishments. I found this profoundly symbolic and was further inspired to complete the book.

I cannot speak for the Whitman sisters. Nobody can. This is an important point to make as theories that attempt to make totalizing statements that claim universal applicability are, by their very nature, suspect.[17] Rather, I can analyze the information and draw conclusions based on the evidence. And although I cannot speak their voices, my job as a scholar is to provide an accurate, detailed analytical account so that scholarship may be furthered and so that we may learn from their stories. It is also important to state that this book is my analysis of the materials, informed by my biases, my position as a black female scholar at this particular time, and my understanding of the constructions of truth and history. I am hopeful that the next scholar who approaches this material will bring a new perspective and be able to further expand the work begun here. In this book I attempt to apply a theoretical analysis to the Whitman sisters' work in order to interrogate the ways in which they illuminate, contradict, and complicate issues of identity politics at the beginning of the twentieth century in terms of the constructions of race, gender, and class.

So that they are not silenced, I reclaim their history. So that they are not silenced, I call out their names. So that they are not silenced, I state their particulars. This book is intended for those of us who need this history in order to survive, so that we, as a community, may gather and remember, to share our inheritance and learn from the past. My hope is that more scholars will take up the challenge to write forgotten women of color back into history.

Introduction

AT THE DAWN OF THE TWENTIETH CENTURY, professional African American performers were employed primarily in vaudeville, a line of work that combined the theatrical traditions of variety, minstrelsy, and road shows. With a few notable exceptions, these performers were prohibited from touring on white vaudeville circuits, and it was not until the 1910s and 1920s that black vaudeville circuits like the Theatre Owners' Booking Association (Toby) stepped in to fill the market by developing and promoting black talent and catering to black audiences. Studying these early pioneers gives us insight into an important legacy of American theater, especially the ways in which racism operated and was confronted in the entertainment industry. As early African American performers honed their craft, they helped pave the way for others by battling institutionalized racism and restrictions placed on black artistic expression. Barred from portraying serious dramatic roles, African American performers worked in the only genres available to them, comedy and musicals, and transcended expectations.

Black female performers faced additional challenges in the ample racism, sexism, and classism of the time. These women's struggles reflected national power politics; beliefs about the place of black women in the larger social framework greatly influenced the career opportunities available to African American female performing artists. In this book, I examine the ways in which the Whitman Sisters refigured race, class, and gender in order to succeed in show business.

This analysis of the Whitman Sisters' work is intended for both dance and theater scholars as well as scholars interested in African American studies. As such, this book functions at the intersections of these scholarly traditions, where black women performed in American theatrical productions, and speaks to these groups who don't speak often enough to each other. I believe that each field can inform and enrich the others, and I hope to create an open space for dialogue. Because I am writing for these different readers, I use some basic terms and figures which may well be familiar to one group, while novel to another group. At the risk of overexplaining, I clarify terms liberally. Although I assume a degree of familiarity with the broader subjects and theories, I try to point out resources for further study of general background information that may be helpful to those less familiar with certain concepts.

The seven-page chapter in *Jazz Dance* was the most extensive scholarly study of the Whitman Sisters prior to this book. The Stearnses based their work on performer interviews, and although their work is invaluable, they did not comprehensively examine the myriad contributions of the Whitman Sisters to the entertainment industry, nor did they attempt to provide in-depth social, historical or political analyses of the group. Other scholarly texts on black theater and dance like *African American Theatre: An Historical and Critical Analysis* by Samuel A. Hay[1] and *Black Dance* by Edward Thorpe[2] give only cursory mentions of the group. More often, the Whitman Sisters has been completely left out of the discourse.[3] Even *Dusky Maidens: The Odyssey of the Early Black Dramatic Actress*, a book that purports to be an extensive analysis of the major black female figures in the entertainment industry during the early twentieth century, fails to mention the Whitman Sisters. In defense of many of these texts, their scope, usually a broad survey of black entertainment history, prevents their authors from focusing deeply on any particular group. This is further testament to the need for advanced research in this area. By focusing on one group, I am able to offer a more complete discourse on a topic that merits in-depth study.

As I stated above, the Whitman sisters—Mabel, Alberta, Essie, and Alice—are, like many other early black entertainers, for the most part egregiously absent from general theater and dance history texts. Negro vaudeville is also a neglected subject in scholarship on black theater, as more focus is usually placed on the somewhat contemporaneous 1920s Harlem Renaissance movement.[4] Although scholars have examined folk culture as part of the Harlem Renaissance and the broader history of African American culture,[5] little attention has been paid to the popular culture of black vaudeville. Oversights like these exemplify a major challenge facing African American theater and dance scholars: producing recuperative, analytic history. As James V. Hatch states, "Black American theater history has not yet been assimilated into our mainstream bibliographies, directories, biographies, scholarly journals, and history texts."[6] Regardless of whether we favor this type of assimilation, excluding minority theater history ensures that the story of American theater will not be fully told. It is imperative that the rich, diverse history of African American performance be taught to our students in more than a diluted gloss. Detailed, complex historical studies must be created. By focusing on the Whitman Sisters as major early-twentieth-century artists, I participate in the project of reclaiming and expanding the African American theatrical tradition as well as enriching two fields often seen as distinct, African American Theater and American Theater histories. As such, I hope this book functions as a methodological example for subsequent scholars interested in African American theater and dance scholarship.

In *Notable Black Women*, Robert L. Johns argues that the Whitman Sisters' relative obscurity derives in part from the fact that the company's strengths were in the area of dance, a field of study even more neglected than music or theater.[7] Although the sisters have survived more in the literature of dance than theater or music, they made significant contributions to all three genres. Perhaps dance history has held onto their stories more closely because of the tendency of dance histories to rely upon genealogical trees of who studied with whom, and the Whitman Sisters taught many dancers who later became famous. Indeed, the chapter in *Jazz Dance* consists mainly of interviews with performers who got an early opportunity with the Whitman Sisters. Their protégés would not let their names be completely erased from national memory. Although no film or audio recording of their work survives, those who witnessed their skill can and have attested to their greatness. Also, many personal documents, scrapbooks, pictures, and other items that were in the family's possession were destroyed by fire in their Chicago home in 1963. The sisters' home in Chicago was torn down. A car dealership exists there now. A fire also destroyed their father's papers in their childhood home in Atlanta. That house was torn down for a highway.

Another reason for their absence in scholarship is the fact that vaudeville is a neglected field of study within theater history. Scholars have reinforced a high/low dichotomy that privileges "serious" drama above forms like musicals, melodrama, and vaudeville. Also, according to Johns, although the sisters appeared on major white touring circuits early in their careers, they devoted themselves for the most part to entertaining black audiences, toured the South extensively and based their operations in Chicago, away from the entertainment center of New York.[8] This dedication to African Americans in areas other than New York may have cost them national fame, for had they stayed on the white circuits and moved to New York (which they were invited to do), they might have garnered fame on the order of the well-known dancer and comedian Bert Williams, the first African American to appear in the Ziegfield Follies and the breaker of many color barriers.[9] Although some of Williams' black contemporaries considered his move to the white stage a betrayal of his race, it helped secure for Williams a place in American theater history books.[10]

The factors mentioned above have all contributed to the neglect of the Whitman Sisters by theater historians. As such, I needed to do much of the preliminary work compiling primary and secondary resources. I was able to find a handful of archives with source materials, including the New York Public Library, Billie Rose Collection, the Hatch-Billops Collection, and the Jazz Institute at Rutgers. I spent more than a year in archives, leafing through old, often unindexed newspapers searching for a mention of the sisters. I found that although buried, primary documentation on the Whitmans' careers could be located with sufficient digging.

❖   ❖   ❖

I collected historical data by compiling and analyzing reviews. However, in my research, I confronted one of the major obstacles facing African American theater and dance scholars, namely lost and hidden primary sources. As I stated above, institutionalized racism and the undervaluing of African American cultural artifacts have meant that many primary documents have been lost, buried, or poorly recorded. Therefore, my research process involved not only visiting archives around the country and consulting sources such as reviews, biographies, and autobiographies of artists who worked with the sisters, but also researching contextual issues in order to support speculation about areas for which no direct evidence exists.

As I stated earlier, the bibliography of *Jazz Dance* shows that most of the Stearnses' information on the Whitman Sisters came from personal interviews with people who worked with the Whitmans on the circuit. Though further interviews are not possible—most of these people have since passed away—I was able to reexamine the Stearnses' interview notes, focusing on the agenda set out for this book. I was able to discuss my work with many scholars, informing them of the sisters' work and discussing possible implications and areas for speculation. Also, I was fortunate enough to obtain firsthand accounts from newspaper articles and interviews.

The reviews I found in small black newspapers proved to be the most valuable resources as they added the most new insight into the sisters' careers. I found announcements of where the Whitman Sisters were next appearing, which led me to scan local black papers in that area, often turning up a review of a performance and sometimes an announcement of the next town on the tour. In this way, I was able to piece together a chronology that traces the Whitman sisters' activities over the years. Many reviewers also offered descriptions of the look and feel of the performances, gave clues as to the ways in which the troupe was received by its audiences, and discussed the sisters' off-stage activities. Although there are some performances which received only an announcement instead of a review, the reviews that we do have paint a detailed picture of the sisters' work.

I feel compelled to say a word about using reviews as sources in order to explain the ways in which I am reading my source materials. I have found that reviews of black performances in major papers must be read with prudence. Because many vaudeville reviews were written by white men, turn-of-the-century racial politics must be considered. As Woll points out, it is difficult to use reviews by white critics to reconstruct the history of black theater.[11] White critics for the major newspapers held the success or failure of each new show in their hands. Oftentimes, these white critics discouraged ambition in black vaudeville shows and frequently gave good reviews only to shows that satisfied their own preconceptions and stereotypes.[12] Indeed, it is clear that these reviewers, if they reviewed black shows at all, often read performances differently from black critics.[13]

Certainly, individual spectator response to the dancing in these shows was influenced in part by race. Some white critics decried the danger to society and immorality of African-based dance styles that were fast-paced, loose-limbed, and pelvic-based isolations.[14] Reviews of black performances (especially black women's performances) at this time by white male reviewers tended to focus on the explicit, the exotic, and the erotic body, valuing only that which reinforced what was believed to be the only roles African Americans were capable of performing. The naturally savage black dancer imbued with animalistic instincts was considered by white reviewers to be a threat to a more moralistic Eurocentric lifestyle.[15] At the same time, some black critics applauded the identification, creation, and perpetuation of a vernacular black aesthetic.[16] At any rate, the subsequent black dance craze of the 1920s in both white and black communities is undeniable proof that African American dance styles informed the national consciousness. As early agents of black dance styles, the Whitman Sisters played a major role in creating and popularizing the idioms of black dance for a wide variety of spectators. The sisters had to carefully cultivate an image that dissuaded an immoral reading of their work and promoted them as positive representatives of their race. By doing this, the Whitman Sisters act was able to become one of the greatest success stories of Negro vaudeville.

In my research, I found that since very few white critics for major newspapers reviewed the Whitman Sisters shows, even these suspect accounts were scarce. Black female performers like the Hyer Sisters and the famous Sissieretta Jones (the Black Patti) were reviewed more by white critics because they sang operas, an allegedly higher form of performance than the Whitmans Sisters', and were not "mere Jubilee singers."[17] Sissieretta Jones even performed in the White House and before England's royal family. The Whitman Sisters, however, performed popular shows mainly for black audiences. Therefore, their names did not appear in popular white presses and only occasionally in smaller white presses. This practice is another type of silencing to which the Whitman Sisters were subjected and part of the reason they are missing from so many narratives of theater history. Even though for a good part of the company's early years it toured on white circuits and was very popular with these audiences (according to reviews in black newspapers and interviews), it was nonetheless ignored by most white critics. This lack of coverage may be seen as a form of censorship perhaps intended to diminish the sisters' popularity and importance on the white vaudeville stage where they competed with white performers. Like discouraging ambition, this practice was calculated in such a way as to assure that black performers did not overstep what white critics deemed were their bounds.

Fortunately, I was able to find quite a few reviews of Whitman Sisters shows in smaller black papers which I believe give accurate accounts of regional public reception. I have used these extensively, as well as several firsthand accounts, to provide black perspectives on the Whitman Sisters' work. Reviews of black entertainment increased in number and frequency as the years passed and black minstrelsy and vaudeville became more popular. Most of the black performers at the end of the nineteenth century were men, but by the 1880s black female minstrels were being hired in increasing numbers, and the standards for black female performances were being set, especially with the establishment of the black dancing girl. The Hyer Sisters, Black Patti's Troubadours, and the Whitman Sisters received more coverage in the press than individual black female performers.

On a few occasions, eldest sister Mabel Whitman also spoke to the press, who quoted her at length, giving the reader insight into the history of the group, the activities of the performers, and their audiences' reception as she saw it.

In reading these reviews and accounts of the performances from various sources, I recognize that one cannot make sweeping claims about audience reception based on several reviews. I also recognize that there were multiple spectatorships in operation during Whitman Sisters shows and that a white man may have experienced a show differently from a black woman. There were also regional differences in reception; New York audiences may have experienced, for example, a plantation number differently than an Atlanta audience might. Also, the performers probably "played" differently to different audiences, so that a hip swing was slightly less suggestive during a show at a local church than it was at the popular theater. One of my goals in this book is to use in-depth analysis of the primary and secondary source materials to address the many layers of performance at work in these shows. In combining sentimental ballads, cross-dressing, and blackface numbers into one performance bill, the sisters not only appealed to different tastes, they also commented on certain assumptions about race, gender, and class, which individual audience members picked up on to varying degrees. It must be noted, though, that because the Whitman Sisters tried to racially integrate their audiences as much as possible, they probably did not make drastic repertory changes based on geography or how they thought an audience might receive the show. Rather, it is more likely that there were different levels of awareness that informed different spectators' experiences. For example, a black spectator may pick up on the comment on racial identity when the sisters passed for white more so than a white audience member might have because it was probably a more immediate part of the black spectator's reality.

Unfortunately, due to missing documentation, I was occasionally forced to speculate based on what we know of the times and other vaudeville performers' practices in order to fill in the gaps of the chronology. For example, we do not have historical records detailing the sisters' tours abroad. We know that early in their careers, Mabel and Essie Whitman toured abroad with their mother, Caddie, as a chaperone. We do not know which countries they toured, but by examining what contemporaneous black performers had to say about touring abroad and countries that were friendly to African American performers, we can surmise that the two sisters played to French, English, and perhaps Russian audiences.

Nor do we have programs of the performances which would give us details about the order in which acts occurred. In the reconstruction of a possible performance that I give, all of the details about what happened during a show are taken from accounts by performers, but I speculate on the order. In other words, I make certain claims about the way acts probably followed each other based on who was in them (giving performers enough time to make a costume change), the popularity of certain types of performances (nobody wanted to follow a really popular act, so perhaps a lesser-known performer was given this spot), and the typical arch of a vaudeville show (orchestras often warmed up the audience before a show and the finale was usually a big number with all company members).

As well as using contextual analysis of primary and secondary materials to give a more comprehensive account of the Whitman sisters' accomplishments, I also use several types of analytical theory to draw conclusions about the significance of their work. These theories are needed to engage in a more sophisticated level of analysis beyond description. It is through theory that I am able to make more advanced, scholarly claims about the social implications of their repertory choices and their management practices. I use black feminist theories, feminist theories of performance, and theories on class and popular culture to analyze the many layers of performance in which the Whitman Sisters participated, on and off stage. It is beyond the scope of this book to address every tenet of each theoretical discourse. Rather, I limit my use to theories with particular epistemological bearing on the subjects at hand, always focusing on the goal of providing an accurate portrayal of the Whitman Sisters.

Black feminist theories that offer insight into the complex interconnectedness of political issues of race, gender, and class are vital to this study. Scholars have developed analytical methodologies which allow the complexities of race, gender and class to be factors in critical inquiry.[18] Womanists are also now beginning to fully articulate their position as related to more established forms of criticism, and although not yet completely developed, womanist theories allow me to fill in gaps in scholarship as it concerns women of color and performance. Alice Walker defines womanism in *In Search of Our Mother's Gardens*. She tells us that womanists are black feminists or feminists of color who are "outrageous, audacious, courageous or willful"; who seek political empowerment; who affirm women's strength; who appreciate the cultural production of all women of color; and who are universally "committed to the survival and wholeness of entire people, male *and* female."[19]

Although the Whitman Sisters probably would not have used the terms *black feminist* or *womanist* to describe their work, it is nonetheless important to use these concepts to understand their place in history as part of the "self-conscious struggle that empowers women and men to actualize a humanist vision of community."[20] Collins reminds us that, "reclaiming the Black women's intellectual tradition involves examining the everyday ideas of Black women not previously considered intellectuals."[21]

I use these theories as analytical tools but by no means do I imply any prescriptive conclusions. As Barbara Christian warns, "In the race for theory, feminists eager to enter the halls of power have attempted their own prescriptions . . . [a]nd seldom do feminist theorists take into account the complexity of life."[22] I use black feminist theory in order to recognize patterns, to understand intricacies and to draw conclusions about the Whitman Sisters' work, not to prescribe totalizing formulas applicable to all black women.

This work also draws from the field of feminist performance theory, a field that often neglects to analyze issues of race in addition to gender and class in performance. As theorists such as Sue-Ellen Case and Gayle Austin admit,[23] no major work has been written in this field that thoroughly addresses race as well as gender. Most comprehensive theories of gender and performance address the cultural production of white women in the United States, England, and Canada. Although many of these studies acknowledge the lack of attention paid to minority women and make a cursory attempt to address racial issues, such treatment is usually brief and inadequate. Indeed, as Higginbotham reminds us, feminist scholars interested in women's history must take up the challenge to figure race more prominently into the analysis of power. She describes three strategies which I use in this study. They are: (1) defining the construction and "technologies" of race as well as those of gender and sexuality; (2) exposing the role of race as a metalanguage with a lasting effect on social and power relations; and (3) recognizing race as providing sites of dialogic exchange and contestation.[24]

This book draws from the methodological traditions of feminist performance scholarship in that it reexamines and applies specifically to black female performers theories laid out by feminist performance scholars.[25] As such, we are able to see how certain theories illuminate the study and others need to be modified to accommodate an analysis of previously neglected subjects of study, in this case African American women. An example of the ways in which this methodological practice is utilized is drawn from Elaine Aston's book *An Introduction to Feminism and Theatre*, in which she discusses the feminist concept of women "hidden from history."[26] This concept has prompted many feminist theater scholars to investigate why and how women have been buried by man-made theater history. It has also initiated a tradition of feminist scholarship devoted to the recovery of "lost" female figures. This theory is also articulated by black feminist theorists and black historians. As mentioned earlier, VèVè Clark articulates a theory of archeology to approach black figures hidden from history.[27] And as Carter G. Woodson discussed in 1933, African Americans have been systematically, institutionally excluded from history. This leads not only to the devaluation and detriment of the black race but also perpetuates worldwide ignorance.

"In history, of course, the Negro had no place in this curriculum."[28] Using these different approaches in tandem instead of in opposition grants us a richer understanding of African American women's work and place in history. We are able to analyze the ways in which people are hidden and the ways in which they can transcend this state.

The work is also significant to the study of popular culture because by recovering pioneers of black popular culture we increase our knowledge of the relationship between African American and Euro-American popular cultural practices and the ways in which the Whitman Sisters capitalized on, as well as influenced, the established traditions of vaudeville. Theories of popular culture, especially those as articulated by Lawrence Levine, focusing on class and status in popular entertainment, allow me to analyze the Whitman Sisters as vaudevillians and give me the language to discuss the degree to which the Whitman Sisters affected and were affected by certain social dynamics. For example, one fascinating aspect of the Whitman sisters' work that theories of popular culture allowed me to investigate was their desire to promote their shows as "high-class" entertainment. As I discuss later, Lawrence Levine tells us that the desire to promote entertainment as respectable often results when cultures bifurcate performance into high/low categories and attach value judgments to each.[29]

In the case of the Whitman sisters, this is further complicated when issues of class are figured with issues of race and gender. I use articulations by scholars of African American studies, like Evelyn Brooks Higginbotham and Kevin Gaines, who speak on class in order to probe these issues. The sisters were particularly vested in a respectable image for the company because women (especially black women) in theater at the time were not typically considered respectable. Victorian notions of (white) "true womanhood" were prevalent, and many middle-class black women tried to fit into these idealized images, fighting the hegemony's labels categorizing them as ignorant, immoral, and inferior. Black female entertainers such as the Whitman sisters also had to fight the age-old stigma attached to women in show business of being loose and base, especially since they were not under the auspices of a male manager. The Whitman sisters promoted their show as a high-class road show and were full participants in the practice of racial uplift. As manager of the Whitman Sisters, Mabel combated stereotypes of race and gender by promoting the company as a classy, respectable enterprise run by well-educated black businesswomen.

By interrogating the primary materials I found as well as the secondary sources, and by filling in the gaps in their stories using contextual and theoretical analysis, I move well beyond the work begun by the Stearnses.

I examine the materials critically and draw conclusions about the Whitman Sisters' contribution to American theater and dance.

I argue that because the Whitman Sisters assumed responsibility for the repertory and management of the company, they gained control over not only the means but also the ends of their production. By destabilizing fictions of race and gender identity while upholding high-class images and challenging audience members, producers, and theater owners to reevaluate their expectations and accepted norms, these women succeeded in claiming a degree of agency over their bodies and transforming the vaudeville stage into a site of resistance. They resisted stereotypes that were developed to distort their images, and they resisted society's restrictions on what they as black women could accomplish. Although the Whitman Sisters operated prior to the emergence of feminist movements in theater, the troupe challenged male patriarchal notions of black womanhood in theater and made significant advances in the struggle for black female equality through their repertory and business procedures. They thus may be said to have accomplished black feminist/womanist goals.

The Whitman Sisters troupe was one of the most important vaudeville organizations at the turn of the century, led by four of the most formidable black women in Negro vaudeville. These women succeeded in breaking many of the barriers for black women in show business and helped pave the way in the entertainment industry for subsequent black performers. In terms of management, Mabel Whitman was the only black female manager at the time; she garnered the best acts, and was a champion for desegregating theaters and fighting corruption in the vaudeville industry. As to repertory, the sisters challenged representations of race by slipping in and out of racial identity, passing for both white and black. Alberta Whitman also challenged gender representations by convincingly cross-dressing, while Alice capitalized on her image as an adorable baby doll. As evidence of the sisters' influence, later stars such as singer Ethel Waters, dancer Bill Robinson, musician Count Basie, and dancer Aaron Palmer credit the Whitman sisters for guiding them to success through their "maternal" style of management. The Whitman Sisters can therefore be said to be one of the most important forces in Negro vaudeville and therefore deserve a prominent place in American and world theater history. Knowledge of their story as part of Negro vaudeville helps us to better understand later genres of black and American performances. In this book, I argue that the Whitman Sisters manipulated their race, gender, and class to resist hegemonic forces while achieving success; by maintaining a respectable image, they were able to challenge fictions of identity in terms of race and gender.

Again, I support this argument by reconstructing and analyzing the history of the Whitman Sisters using primary and secondary materials as well as utilizing black feminist/womanist theories, feminist performance theories, and theories of class and popular culture. I access all of these sources in order to draw a complete picture of the Whitman Sisters' performance dynamic.

The three remaining chapters in this book are arranged as a combination of historical narrative and analytical exegesis. In chapter two, I detail the Whitman Sisters' early years, explaining theatrical influences and historically situating their entrance into the theatrical industry. I hope to lay the groundwork in this chapter for the reader by painting a complete picture of the early years before delving into theoretical arguments. I argue that they drew from not only Euro-American traditions and the short history of African Americans on stage, but also from the long tradition of African American performance. I also reconstruct a possible show based on personal accounts and reviews to give the reader a stronger image of what was happening in a Whitman Sisters show.

In chapter three, I lay out the historical evidence and theoretical support to substantiate my claims regarding the ways in which the Whitman sisters negotiated race and gender. I argue that in their repertory and off-stage business dealings, the Whitman Sisters destabilized race and gender norms by upholding certain standards about class, respectability, and uplift. I conclude this chapter by examining the management practices that led to the company's success, continuing my arguments about race, class, and gender.

In the fourth and final chapter, I resume the narrative begun in chapter two and examine the later years of the Whitmans' careers. I show how in these years, on the Toby circuit and during the Depression, the Whitman sisters continued to maintain their high standards despite the decline of the company.

This book represents the most comprehensive study of primary and secondary documentation on the Whitman Sisters, the most extensive historical account of their lives and work, and the most in-depth analysis of their performances and practices. Again, my hope is that this work can serve as a base for further research and inspire other scholars to take up the task of writing a more complete and accurate theater and dance history.

This work brings the disparate information about the Whitman Sisters into one place and focuses on recovering and analyzing the sisters as "hidden" black female performers, writing them back into theater and dance history as key forces in the development of early American entertainment. The Whitman sisters' stories may have been hidden for far too long, but they are not lost.

Setting the Stage:
Beginnings, Influences, And a
Performance Reconstruction

For the past two weeks this city has been musically electrified by some of the greatest musical artists in this country. Notwithstanding Barnum and Bailey's Circus, Buffalo Bill and other great productions, the concerts that have been given by the Whitman Sisters in the several churches have been attended by overflowing houses.

These young ladies are natural-born singers, and their renditions of their musical numbers certainly electrify their audiences.[1]

BEGINNINGS

Little did the African Methodist Episcopal minister Reverend Albery Allson Whitman know when he gave singing and dancing lessons to his three daughters (Mabel, ca. 1880–1942; Essie, ca. 1882–1963; and Alberta, ca. 1888–1964) that they would go on to form one of the most successful Negro vaudeville troupes in history. While living in Missouri, Kansas, and Georgia he taught them the double shuffle (only for exercise, he insisted) and religious songs, with the intent that the girls would accompany him on evangelical tours and church benefits.[2] The three girls, sang, danced, and played the guitar while he preached. Although we do not have programs from these early performances, nor do we have any descriptions of what these shows were like, we can nonetheless surmise that the repertory probably consisted mostly of singing spirituals. The dancing probably focused on portraying the girls as cute tappers and would have steered clear of the dance styles popular on the stage at the time. The syncopated rhythms of some spirituals, with which congregations were undoubtedly familiar through their own hand-clapping, could easily have been translated to tap. There were certain styles that were probably less welcome in religious settings, like kicklines, shimmies, and any movement that isolated the lower half of the body. These more popular forms, as well as dramatic skits and comedy routines, would not become a part of the Whitman sisters' repertoire until later. In the church setting, however, they had their first lessons in performance, became comfortable in front of spectators and began to learn how to entertain an audience.[3]

The Whitman Sisters' dance beginnings as church performers is unusual. Although jubilee singers usually began singing in churches, the fact that the girls also danced is significant and was not the norm in Southern black churches.[4] In fact, most forms of popular dance entertainment were considered low and had no proper place in the church. In *The Ghost Walks: A Chronological History of Blacks in Show Business, 1865-1910*,[5] no other dancers are mentioned as performing in churches. The fact that the Whitman sisters' father was a preacher probably helped protect the girls from getting a less-than-respectable reputation.[6] The A.M.E. church was an extremely powerful and influential force in the lives of many African Americans at this time and was second only to the National Baptist Convention in membership among African Americans.[7] As in other black denominations, the A.M.E. church was dedicated not only to saving the eternal souls of its members but also to improving their earthly lots by promoting education and civility as well as piety. Thus, any dancing presented by the young Whitman sisters must have been in line with the church's values. By the fact that the girls were well received, we can safely assume that hip isolations were probably kept to a minimum when the girls danced. When they were young, the sisters could use the fact that they were cute as a defense against seeming indiscretions. When they got older, they needed more complex negotiations when they played church engagements.[8]

It is likely that Reverend Whitman saw the Fisk Jubilee Singers in concert at Wilberforce University in Wilberforce, Ohio, when he was studying there in 1871 and was inspired to combine concertized sacred music with his preaching. The spirituals of the Fisk University students in the 1870s were the first undeniably black music idiom to reach the American concert stage, and their sorrow songs of bondage tugged at Victorian heartstrings throughout the United States and Europe.[9] While continuing a religious tradition, these songs crossed over to the entertainment industry and soon became a staple of minstrel shows, folk choruses, and black concert companies.[10] Unlike dance, many musical traditions in the black church have influenced African American theater, including "the black church's syncopated music, call-response between leader and congregation, spontaneous testimonies, and possession by the spirit."[11] As ritual becomes commercial, "the church has been the path to professional careers in theatre."[12] Thus, the Whitman Sisters' musical roots in sacred music are less unusual than the company's dance roots in church performances.

In addition to being inspired by the Fisk Jubilee Singers, the Whitman sisters may have taken a cue from the Hyer sisters, who began touring the country with their stage plays and musical reviews in 1876. For 30 years, Anna Madah and Emma Louise Hyer had a "combination" or touring company that combined different acts. The Whitman sisters were undoubtedly well aware of the Hyers as they were very well reviewed in the black press, though there is no evidence to suggest that they ever got to see a Hyer Sisters show—the Hyers never played in the Whitmans' hometown or in a location close to their home. Like the Whitman sisters, the Hyers also started out their show business careers singing under the management of their father. Anna Madah and Emma Louise Hyer became the first black women to find success on the American stage.[13] Their shows emphasized racial themes similar to the afterpieces of minstrelsy in which a short plantation skit would be acted out. Their production of *Out of Bondage* (1890) was the first musical show to be produced by a black organization, thus signaling the transition from minstrelsy to black musical comedy in black entertainment. But by 1893 the Hyer sisters had announced that they were leaving the stage. Six years later, the Whitman sisters came onto the scene and pleased audiences black and white, male and female, rich and poor, all across the nation. At a time when most sibling acts were brother teams, the Hyers and the Whitmans were showing America that sisters were just as capable.

❖ ❖ ❖

In order to further place the Whitman sisters work in context, it is important to describe what was happening in the country at the same time. In 1899, American imperialism was still being waged against peoples of color. The United States was coming out of the Spanish-American War; Filipino guerrilla fighters staged insurrections against the United States for the island's independence; there were 85 recorded lynchings in the South, in response to which the National Afro-American Council called for a day of fasting as protest. Ida B. Wells Barnett was active in her antilynching campaigns. At this time, African Americans were subject not only to lynchings but to other forms of violence, disfranchisement, legalized segregation, and the economic enslavement of sharecropping. The first African American learned society, the American Negro Academy, founded by Alexander Crummell, was in its second year. Its presidents over the years would be Alexander Crummell, W. E. B. Du Bois, Archibald Grimké, John W. Cromwell, and Arthur Schomburg. Also in its second year was the National Association of Colored Women. Organized with the help of Mary Church Terrell, this organization would go on to sponsor many social reforms and educational programs.

At the same time, African Americans were making significant inroads into the popular entertainment industry. The famous comedians Bert Williams and George Walker began their ten-year collaboration with the show *The Policy Makers;* Eubie Blake composed "Charleston Rag"; and bandleader and composer Duke Ellington, musician Noble Sissle, and blues performer and composer Tommy Dorsey were born.

Also in 1899, two of the young Whitman sisters first stepped onto the stage. Mabel Whitman, age 19, and Essie Whitman, age 17, created their own repertory of jubilee songs, formed an act and hired a hall.[14] They added a more popular style to the jubilee songs, thus blending the styles. Songwriter Perry Bradford claims: "Their swinging style was new in spiritual singing."[15] Seeing the opportunities available in branching out beyond religious songs, Mabel and Essie next made the transition to singing harmony and more popular songs like "Adam Never Had No Mammy" and "Little Black Me."[16] Mabel was noted to have a beautiful voice, but it was Essie's contralto that significantly impressed critics, and she soon received recognition for having the "lowest contralto voice on record."[17]

Figure 1 shows Mabel with dark hair and Essie with lighter hair. This publicity shot is probably intended for the sisters' jubilee concert audience. Note the emphasis on music and the lack of a theatrical setting that exists in later photographs of the Whitman Sister's company.

George Walker, the famous comedian and a neighbor of the Whitmans in Lawrence, Kansas, returned to their hometown after his first trip to the East Coast and attempted to sponsor Mabel and Essie on a trip to New York in order to promote the start of their professional careers. Reverend Whitman objected, however. Instead, the two older sisters continued their

Figure 1. Mabel and Essie Whitman.
Reproduced by kind permission of Ernestine Lucas.

Figure 2. Alberta Whitman.
Reproduced by kind permission of Ernestine Lucas.

education in Lawrence.[18] Although they did not go to New York with George Walker, they did continue to perform in the South. Will Accooe, a musical director who worked on many black musical comedy productions like *A Trip to Coontown*, *The Cannibal King*, and *The Sons of Ham*, created a short singing and dancing skit for Essie and Mabel, and in 1899, billed as the Danzette Sisters, they toured from Missouri to Florida.[19] They traveled throughout the South under the personal management of their mother, Caddie Whitman.[20] Shortly after returning from an evangelical tour with their father, they made their professional debut as a "filler" for an open spot on the bill at the Orpheum theater in Kansas City. According to Mabel they were "an instantaneous hit."[21] Mr. Lehman, manager of the Orpheum, succeeded where Walker had failed and after much trouble obtained permission from Reverend Whitman to sign the sisters to tour the Orpheum and Kohl & Castle circuits with a chaperone. On this tour, they appeared on the same bills with white vaudevillians like Joseph Jart, Carrie DeMar, Cater DeHaven, Baby Lund, the Four Cohans, Jones and Grant, Gracie Emmett, Jesse Dandy, thus making the Danzette Sisters one of the few black vaudeville groups to tour on predominantly white circuits.[22] Soon after, Caddie chaperoned them on a tour abroad and, upon returning home, the third sister, Alberta, joined the act. Figure 2 shows a picture of Alberta Whitman. Because the cities to which they toured are not known, efforts to recuperate this part of the history have been unproductive at this point; nonetheless, from examining the practices of other touring performers we can surmise that they probably brought their musical renditions to Europe, especially France and England, where there was less race prejudice. Sissieretta Jones, head of the famous Black Patti's Troubadours, discussed the treatment black performers could expect to receive in Europe:

> In Europe there is no prejudice against my race. It matters not to them what is the color of an artist's skin. If a man or woman is a great actor, or a great musician, or a great singer, they will extend a warm welcome, no matter whether he be Jew or Greek or Gentile. It is the soul they see, not the color of his skin.[23]

According to Whitman relative Ernestine Lucas the sisters gave a command performance before King George V and other members of the British monarchy. Librarians at the Royal Archives were unable to find information about the performance, but claimed that the sisters may have appeared as part of one of the Command Performances in aid of the Variety Artistes Benevolent Fund.[24]

The Whitman sisters may have also toured Australia, as did O. M. McAdoo's Minstrels, or Russia, as did Ira Aldridge; however, these destinations are less likely considering the fact that the troupe was very young and these destinations were considerably expensive. South Africa was known as a destination with severe race prejudice—so severe that when the Meredith Sisters toured the area they billed themselves as American Indian Squaws.[25] Many contemporaneous African American performers went abroad to perform in less racially hostile countries where they were more respected as performers than in America.[26] Not surprisingly, some of these performers chose not to return to America, but as I will discuss below, the Whitman Sisters were able to succeed in this country, especially in African American communities.

Although the historical documents about their mother, Caddie, are even sparser than those for the sisters, it is important to observe that chaperoning the girls around the United States and abroad was an extraordinary act at the time. Rather than hire a manager, typically a white man, Caddie assumed managerial responsibilities herself, surely took on financial risk, and chanced incurring a bad reputation for herself and her daughters.[27]

Though extant records of the girls' careers directly after the tour abroad do not list specific acts and we do not know who was managing the group and determining their material, we can surmise that by 1902, when the girls were appearing on stages as well as in churches, their repertory most likely began to take a new form to meet new audience expectations. We know from examining the programs of other vaudeville troupes that performers other than jubilee singers typically performed in shows that combined a variety of acts. Other performers like the Hyer Sisters and Sissieretta Jones expanded their singing repertory to include other types of popular performance.[28] The Whitmans' repertory probably also shifted from strictly singing to a format more closely akin to vaudeville, combining short skits, dancing, and musical interludes. Alberta was particularly adept at character performances and was well known for her male impersonations.

We do not know Caddie Whitman's opinions of her daughters' move to popular performance, but at least one source speculates that Reverend Whitman probably disliked the idea of his daughters performing anything other than divinely inspired songs. Many other African American popular entertainers, such as Dinah Washington, Bobby Womack, Lou Rawls, and Sam Cook talk of familial disapproval of their career choices.[29] According to Clarence Muse, the Reverend disowned the sisters when they insisted upon a secular repertory. Because Muse does not cite evidence for his speculation, his claims must be recognized as rumor and read with caution.[30] Muse states:

Their father is a minister and they started out doing tableaux in churches to gain money for "rallies." Somewhere along the line they realized the money-making possibilities of what they were doing and branched out into show business. The old man disowned 'em then.[31]

Muse might be using the term "disown" to describe the severity of Reverend Whitman's disapproval.[32] This claim is confounded by the fact that Reverend Whitman is said to have left the sisters $60,000 upon his death.[33] If he had indeed disowned his daughters, one would suppose that he would have left his money to the A.M.E. church or to his alma mater. Ernestine Lucas denies that Reverend Whitman could have left so large a sum of money to the girls. She speculates that the sisters started the rumor to garner more "human interest."[34] Lucas also doubts that the sisters and their father had a falling out:

From everything I've heard about him, he was was [sic] a very sensitive inverted person who hid his feelings and I think that even if he had any antagonism toward them [his daughters] that it wouldn't have come out.[35]

It is probably the case that Reverend Whitman greatly disapproved of his daughters' actions, however. When appearing before a church audience in 1908, Mabel addressed the spectators/congregation and spoke of the admonition the Reverend Whitman gave the girls before his death and how they "struggled to maintain their honor and reputation."[36] The *Washington Bee* reviewer noted that their success with this church audience proved that they were victorious in this endeavor:

The vast audience that cheered this address was an evidence of the esteem and appreciation in which this community holds these young ladies.[37]

Reverend Whitman's feelings were not uncommon at a time when upstanding families (black and white) carefully cultivated respectable images. Show business hardly fell under the rubric of respectability, and in the Deep South at the turn of the century having daughters who contributed to the "immorality" and "vulgarity" of the stage was enough to put any honorable A.M.E. minister to shame.[38]

Reverend Whitman was not a stranger to artistic expression, however. On the contrary, he was a poet of some renown and was considered the most prolific black poet of his time. He published his first poem "Leelah Misled" in

1873 and his last "An Idyll of the South" in 1901. He uses Spenserian stanzas in "The Rape of Florida" (he was the only black poet of his time to do so) and his poem "Not a Man and Yet a Man" was the longest poem ever published by an African American until 1877.[39] Although an orphan by the age of 12, he worked his way from slavery and life as a poor farm boy and plow shop worker after emancipation to become "Poet Laureate of the Negro Race,"[40] publishing seven volumes of poetry. In 1893 he was asked to write a poem for Colored American Day at the Chicago World's Fair. The poem, "Freedom's Triumphant Song," was read by Caddie. Although he had had only about a year of formal schooling himself, he greatly emphasized the importance of education. He worked as a schoolteacher, established churches, and led congregations in Ohio, Kansas, Texas, and Georgia.[41] Though busy with his religious work, the leading African American poet of his day[42] managed to write long, narrative, melodramatic poems. Although Reverend Whitman is rumored to have been first cousin to Walt Whitman,[43] his literary idol was Henry Wadsworth Longfellow, whose poetic skill he aspired to attain.[44]

Poetry, however, was viewed as a respectable endeavor while popular performance (show business) was not. This is an important distinction to make and helps to explain Reverend Whitman's feelings. As I discuss later, respectability and image were vital to the upper echelons of African American society at this juncture, especially for religious families. Reverend Whitman did not live to see his daughters expand their company to more than 20 members and adopt a full vaudeville repertoire. At the age of 50, Reverend Whitman died in his home in Atlanta of pneumonia, with alcoholism probably a contributing factor.[45]

If the $60,000 estate existed,[46] it would have been enough to provide a tidy nest egg for their budding theatrical careers. In 1902, the year after Reverend Whitman's death, The Whitman Sisters' Novelty Company opened at the Grand Opera House in Augusta, Georgia, and received its first major theatrical review:

> These three bright, pretty mulatto girls are the daughters of the pastor of the A.M.E. Church of Atlanta, Ga. They have wonderful voices, that of Essie being the lowest contralto on record. The sisters play banjos and sing coon songs with a smack of the original flavor. Their costuming is elegant; their manner is graceful and their appearance striking in a degree as they are unusually handsome.[47]

The sisters were well on their way to fame. While in New Orleans in the summer of 1904, they changed the name of the company to The Whitman

Sisters' New Orleans Troubadours and began taking on other acts, beginning with the young Willie (later Bill "Bojangles") Robinson. Robinson was born in Richmond, Virginia, in 1878, the son of a machine-shop worker and a choir singer. Raised by his grandmother after being orphaned as a baby, he began dancing in the streets for pennies and by age six was appearing as a hoofer in local beer gardens. He joined the Whitman Sisters at the age of 12 and was an immediate sensation. Robinson would soon make many innovations in tap dancing, including introducing the on-the-toes style, as opposed to the earlier flat-footed Buck and Wing style. Robinson became one of the most famous tap dancers in American history, perfecting a unique style of extremely rhythmic, complex, syncopated footwork.

In 1905, the company moved its base of operation from Atlanta to Chicago, probably as part of the Great Northern Migration of African Americans out of the rural South to the urban North.[48] Between 1890 and 1910, approximately 200,000 African Americans left for the city fleeing farms, economic hardships brought on by the boll weevil, Southern white racism and the threat of lynchings. The North, in contrast, promised opportunity and relative freedom. The Whitman Sisters were probably also seeking freedom and opportunities as well as following their audiences. Although now based in Chicago, the sisters continued to keep strong ties to African American communities in the South.

However, they also gave performances in Northern cities. One of their most significant early accomplishments in this new environment was a several-month tour of black Baptist and A.M.E. churches first in Chicago and then in the Washington, D.C., metropolitan area, with an extended engagement at the Howard Theater in D.C. By 1908, all three sisters were being praised for their musical abilities; Alberta was known to possess a "sweet voice," Mabel had "great musical ability," and Essie was considered "the most wonderful singer in this country."[49]

The fact that the Whitman Sisters chose to perform in churches so soon after their move is significant. They probably wanted to keep their ties to the African American religious communities strong and wanted to counter any stigma that they might receive for leaving the rural South for Northern cities, which were considered by some to be rowdy and dangerous.

The reviews of these shows are revealing in several ways. Not only do they sing the sisters' praises and confirm the popularity and importance of the group, they also speak to the group's loyalty to the community. The reviewer knows the family to be upstanding folks, which increases their entitlement to success. The review of their Chicago tour speaks not only to their success, but also to their respectability as good Christians.

Note that their status in the community contributes to their success as performers:

HEAR WHAT THE PRESS HAS TO SAY.

The Whitman Sisters are making fine runs in Chicago and meeting with great success. This is gratifying and proper; these people are no fakes, but strong, intelligent, Christian people from one of the Negro families in the South, and their plays and renditions have never been surpassed in Chicago. They give more than the worth of the auditor's money in any performance. The Conservator is proud that the good, appreciative people of Chicago are so liberally encouraging this excellent family of talent and push. The Whitman Sisters move on merit and not in cheap gush. While we know these sweet sisters are not struck on The Conservator because we misplaced the picture of one of them, as they thought, in our columns, we know the family and want to see them succeed even if they do not understand us. They are good and intelligent people. Encourage them.[50]

An important part of the Whitman Sisters' images relied on the performances being perceived as high quality by reviewers and not "cheap gush." Only with a high-quality show could the Whitman Sisters attract the upper crust of black society. From the following review of the D.C. church performances we can see that the troupe not only performed jubilee songs, but also brought humor to the hallowed venues as Bill Robinson managed to keep the audiences laughing. If dancing was considered unusual in black churches at this time, then joke telling was even rarer. One can only imagine what these jokes were like since no scripts exist, but it is probably safe to assume that they were not too blue or low brow:

THE WHITMAN SISTERS.

Notwithstanding the excessively warm weather last Wednesday evening, Galbraith Church was crowded to its full capacity. The main auditorium, one-half of which was reserved, and also the gallery was [sic] packed to suffocation with a most distinguished audience to listen to the celebrated Whitman Sisters, who have taken the city by storm with their classic and varied singing. One of the centers of attraction was Master Willie Robinson, who is a genius, and who keeps his hearers in one continuous roar of laughter.[51]

Not only did the performers have to please these audiences with the quality of their performances, they also had to keep their images in terms of appearance, comportment, and manner of speech. The reviewer continues:

> The three sisters were most beautifully dressed last Wednesday evening. Their costumes were more fascinating and attractive. The singing and funny sayings by Miss Mabel and Master Willie Robinson kept the audience in one continuous roar. Miss Essie has a refined stage carriage and her articulation is most perfect.
>
> The Whitman sisters deserve great credit, and especially Miss Mabel, who is the manager. These young ladies deserve to be encouraged.
>
> Their programme is so arranged that it pleases everybody. Their jubilee songs and other selections cannot help but attract, and in many instances tears are brought from the eyes of the audience.[52]

After these church tours, the sisters were then offered positions in the show *The Oyster Man* with the celebrated comedian Ernest Hogan, but refused, opting to continue touring with their own concerts. They also had the honor of being the first black females to play the Greenwald circuit. They went east and composer Will Marion Cook helped them land a spot on the program of a private musical concert held at the Waldorf-Astoria in honor of a New York magistrate, Judge Cary. They then played several major white circuits including the entire Keith & Proctor circuit, all of the Percy C. Williams houses, and the Poli & Fox circuits. They also appeared regularly in the leading theaters in and around New York. In New York, they signed with the Pantages circuit but had to cancel everything west of Denver in order to return to Atlanta to be with their mother in her final days.

Alice Whitman (ca 1900-1969), the youngest sister, who had been caring for their ailing mother in Atlanta, joined the group in 1909 shortly after Caddie Whitman's death.[53] For reasons that are unclear, Mabel then took some of the younger dancing acts from the Troubadours and opened her own "pick" show called *Mabel Whitman and the Dixie Boys.* "Pick" is short for pickaninnies, and these acts consisted of highly talented black child dancers. A single female singer working with picks was very common at this time. Mabel took her cue from the popular practice of white female singers like Sophie Tucker, Eva Tanguay, and Nora Bayes, who surrounded themselves with picks and went on the road. The picks were considered insurance because no matter how the solo singer fared, the kids would almost never flop. Mabel Whitman and the Dixie Boys toured the United States, Europe, and Australia, and were such successes that Mabel was able to send money back to her sisters. As there is no gap in the review chronology for The Whitman Sisters' New Orleans Troubadours, we can assume that the company continued to perform while Mabel was touring with the Dixie Boys. After Mabel's tour, all four women reorganized the company under the name The Whitman Sisters.

The sisters always kept their shows fresh. Sometimes they appeared on the same ticket as companies such as Billy Kersand's Vaudeville Company but they were never upstaged and usually had top billing. By 1910, they had played most of the major vaudeville circuits in the South, East, and North-east—including the Orpheum, Greenwald, Kohl & Castle, Keith & Proctor, Poli & Fox, Pantages, and the Independent Family United—had appeared as an independent group at the best Southern venues, and had well earned the title "The Royalty of Negro Vaudeville."

The sisters were apart only once from this time until their deaths. Between the years 1911 and 1913, Alice left the show temporarily, Mabel did a "single"—performed alone—in Southern houses, and Essie and Alberta formed a small vaudeville group, including the famous picks Aaron and Sammy (Sambo), which toured the Eastern states as a featured act on the Family United circuit.[54] Mabel then formed a small troupe which spent about 20 weeks touring in and around Boston, with Mabel's likeness appearing in the Boston papers along with those of such stars as comedienne Fanny Brice, the comedy team of Joe Weber and Lew Fields, and singer Irene La Tour. The sisters were together again by 1914, along with new company members from two small troupes. On October 24, 1914, the *Washington Bee* discussed the Whitman Sisters:

> The announcement by Manager Andrew J. Thomas last week that the celebrated Whitman Sisters would appear at his theater this week was the signal for the turn-out of all Washington Monday night to greet them. It is quite evident that they are popular favorites in this city because they had a full house at the American Theater, except one night, when the storm prevented the people from turning out. . . . However, the crowd that greeted the Whitman Sisters at the Howard Monday night was unprecedented. Every available space or anywhere a person was able to squeeze in was occupied Monday night.[55]

In 1918, Mabel looked back on the company's success to that point. In this account she touches on several issues that will become central to my discussion in the next chapter, namely, the group's loyalty to African American audiences and its management successes.

> We consolidated, and since then we have been more than familiar figures in things theatrical, especially on the circuits with which our people are best acquainted. Our record speaks for itself, and there has never been a time when we have not been recognized as the best of all box office attractions. We rely upon no one but ourselves as far as the administration of our business affairs is concerned, and at the same time every effort in our power is made to make each and every engagement booked stand out. In the last remark the managers are fully considered, and, according to the consideration which we always receive from them, we cannot help but think that they feel the same as we.[56]

For the next 30 years, despite wars, the Great Depression, and the decline of vaudeville, the Whitman Sisters troupe managed to avoid most of the hardships of life in show business while entertaining countless black and white audiences in theaters and churches around the country. A class act all the way, the Whitman Sisters performances were always a cut above the average travelling show. They also furthered the African American theater legacy by becoming the greatest incubator of black talent in vaudeville and they would go on to inspire countless African American performers. Buster Brown, talking about when he first became interested in dance, states:

> There was a show that came through Baltimore. They were called the *Whitman Sisters*. There were three sisters that had this big show and on this show they had this juvenile. He must've been about nine or ten years old. His name was Pops Whitman [Albert "Pops" Whitman] And the name of this show was the *Whitman Sisters*. When I seen Pops Whitman dance, I knew right then that that is what I wanted to do. . . . He was a little guy that could—boy! That and the way he was dressed. He had on these long pants. I wasn't even wearing long pants then. He was wearing long pants and this man's suit. Fit him perfectly. That's what I wanted to do. . . . And so as far as first falling in love with dancing, this is the guy that really made me know what I wanted to do. Pops Whitman. He could do anything. He could really dance. He could do a no-hand flip like nobody in the world. This little guy, boy, he could do everything! I think from the time that I saw Pops Whitman, and that was in the early years, before even seeing, before even having—I didn't have the notion then I wanted, I would always wish and hope that

someday I would get into this category—like Pops, with the great suit
and the wonderful dancing. . . .[57]

THEATRICAL INFLUENCES

Where did the Whitman sisters get the material for their acts? Who
influenced their work? What did black vaudeville look and sound like? In
order to fully analyze the Whitman sisters' work, one must take into
consideration the theater history they built upon. An understanding of the
history of black performance in the early twentieth century helps one to
understand the ways in which the Whitman sisters functioned as both
cultural conservators, passing tradition to a younger generation, as well as
cultural innovators, creating repertories that would influence future theater
and dance. Thus, a summary of the important influences and traditions they
inherited is necessary. In this section, I examine the sources from which the
Whitman sisters drew their material and give examples of how this borrowing and influence functioned. This is the groundwork for my in-depth
interrogation in the next chapter, in which I show where the Whitman sisters
made innovations, where they influenced others, where they reinforced
social ideologies and where they resisted cultural standards.

The genre of Negro vaudeville drew from two traditions in performance
history: the African American tradition (divided into theater and drama) and
the Euro-American tradition (extravaganza, revue, and vaudeville). As I will
explain, influences from each can be seen in the Whitmans' work.

When we examine the history of African American performance
traditions that the Whitman sisters inherited, we can see two camps of
thought surrounding these materials. One camp defines performance as
drama, meaning written texts, and the other defines performance as event,
meaning a series of cultural productions, some working from written texts
and others not. The brief history of African Americans on stage working
from written texts must be supplemented with an understanding of the
longer tradition of black performances that were passed down through
generations by means other than writing, including oral heritage, and bodily
memories.[58] If we limit our discussion of African American performance to
the term *drama*, then we must place African American drama's birth in 1816
with the opening of the African Grove Theater in New York and the first
known script written by an African American, *The Drama of King Shotaway*, by
a Mr. Brown.[59] However, if we examine performance as an enacted event,
we may trace the roots of African American performance back past the

nineteenth century to slave traditions rooted in the cultures of the African peoples. The Whitman sisters drew extensively from each of these sources. Not only did they perform written skits, they also performed dances from the African American tradition that were well known, even if the steps were not necessarily written down.

Critics have debated the origins of African American culture and, in the not-too-distant past, some argued for the "lost culture" theory or, as Orlando Patterson calls it, *catastrophism*.[60] Catastrophism holds that when slaves were brought to the United States their cultural slate was wiped clean and that, spongelike, they absorbed "American" culture. For example, in his study on white and Negro spirituals, George Pullen Jackson concludes that there are no traces of African influences in American Negro spirituals and that slaves were taught spirituals by their masters. Therefore, he concludes, Negro spirituals are merely imitations of European folksongs.[61] However, much evidence has surfaced of late to prove the survival of African traditions in African American cultural forms.[62] For example, denouncing claims made by writers such as Jackson, Eileen Southern traces the origins of Negro spirituals directly to the practices of African slaves.[63] The mode of retention was most often collective ancestral memory, whereby oral and corporal memories are transmitted from generation to generation. Many argue that there are different kinds of memory and consciousness. James Hatch divides cultural memory into Africanisms, which are retained and transmitted, and neo-Africanisms, which are learned or, one could argue, relearned.[64] Toni Morrison argues for the importance and authenticity of memory when telling our stories and histories.[65] Regardless of the breakdown, it is clear that African culture in the United States survived and was available to early African American performers such as the Whitman sisters.

Although the history of "professional" stage performance that turn-of-the-century African American performers could look back on was limited, the tradition of black performance off-stage was much vaster. Although usually lacking direct contact with African society, these performers often unconsciously participated in the protection and perpetuation of practices rooted in African culture. Denying theories of cultural destruction, I agree with scholars such as Hatch, Southern, Robinson, and Traylor, who argue that African culture has influenced African American performance tradition. African American slaves did not write down this tradition with pen and paper since reading and writing were forbidden them, but rather recorded their traditions with their voices and bodies and played them back in their songs and dances. Thus, Africanisms were remembered in a collective ancestral memory transmitted through generations, often surreptitiously and in coded forms. It is from this cultural history, including story, music, and dance, that African American artists at the turn of the century could draw.[66]

Scholars such as Dixon-Gottschild, Malone, Fabre, Emery, and the Stearnses have provided evidence of the persistence of dance traditions throughout the African Diaspora.[67] During the Middle Passage, African slaves were brought up from the dark, dank, and crowded hull to the top deck of slave ships, where they were forced, often under threat of the cat-o'-nine-tails—a whip with nine separate leather lashes—to dance in their chains for exercise and for the entertainment of the captain and crew. Since a healthy slave brought the best prices, maintaining good appearances was economically vital to the slave trade. What did these dances look like? It is logical to assume that these slaves drew from the familiar movement vocabulary of the traditional dances of their homeland. Here are the beginnings of African Americans' dual roles as laborers and entertainers.

And how did slaves dance on the plantation when the master called them into the Big House to entertain the family and guests? Again, they danced the dances they knew from their homelands. These styles became influenced by not only the dances of the different ethnic traditions within Africa but also by the traditions of the European cultures that slaves encountered in America.

Slaves also often infused these dances with elements subversive to the institution of slavery, carefully treading the power dynamics so as not to overtly offend and risk retribution. And so, as whites were watching and borrowing from slaves, slaves were watching and borrowing from them. Because these forms were passed down from one generation to the next, they were able to survive in black communities. The Whitman sisters, having spent so much time in Atlanta, were undoubtedly exposed to these forms. Alice told the Stearnses of learning African American dance forms as a child. "As a kid I'd be 'Georgia Hunchin' up and down Auburn Avenue in Atlanta," she said. "Just a little shuffle with taps, but you could move along."[68]

The Cakewalk, for example, was a popular slave dance in which a couple would high step and strut about, subversively mocking the mannerisms and pretensions of the slave master and mistress.[69] The Cakewalk dance figured prominently in the Whitman Sisters' repertory. Alice won many cakewalk contests, and the Whitman Sisters are credited with bringing the Cakewalk to Jackson Field, Georgia. This dance would soon become the first African American vernacular dance popular in both white and black circles, thereby setting the stage for mainstream popularity of black-originated dance idioms.

In times of celebration, dance traditions, religion, music, and stories were transferred among slave cultures at holiday gatherings, festivals, and in areas such as Place Congo in New Orleans, where slaves were permitted to interact more freely. These were times of respite from toil, when slaves of all ages could reinvent freedom, establish a network of communication and perhaps challenge the established order. This topsy-turvy setting, in which slaves and masters could restructure power dynamics so that slaves could move freely about, gather and visit with other slaves, allowed for the transference of culture. During these celebrations, African Americans evoked "a will to remember and the determination to construct an African American memory."[70] In other words, they preserved their heritage by remembering the dances, stories, and music of their ancestors and passed these along to their children.

For example, according to Robert Hinton, "The Ring Shout was perhaps the last example of African religious movement to survive in Afro-American culture."[71] The Ring Shout survived despite some Protestants' branding of dancing (defined as crossing the feet) and drumming as sinful and despite government outlaw of drumming. The Ring Shout did not allow the dancer to cross his or her legs and feet, because the Voodoo tradition at the root of this dance held that anything crossed would keep the "saints" away.[72] As long as the feet did not cross, the movement was not considered sinful dancing and was allowed as a form of religious expression. The Federal Writers' Project quoted Wash Wilson, a Louisiana slave, as saying: "Us 'longed to de church, all right, but dancin' ain't sinful iffen de foots ain't crossed. Us danced at de arbor meetin's but us sho' didn't have us foots crossed!"[73]

When it became clear to slave masters that drums were being used to send messages of potential rebellion from plantation to plantation, they outlawed their use. For example, because of the Stono insurrection, led by a slave named Cato, in 1739, the 1740 Statutes at Large of South Carolina were created:

> And for that as it is absolutely necessary to the safety of this province, that all due care be taken to restrict the wanderings and meetings of Negroes and other slaves, at all times, and more especially on Saturday nights, Sundays, and other holidays, and their using and carrying wooden swords, and other mischievous and dangerous weapons, or using or keeping of drums, horns or other loud instruments which may call together or give sign or notice to one another of their wicked designs and purposes . . . Be it enacted by the authority aforesaid, that

> it shall be lawful for all masters, overseers and other persons whomso-
> ever [sic] to apprehend and take up any Negro or other slave that shall
> be found out of the plantation of his or their master or owner at any
> time, especially on Saturday nights, Sundays or other holidays, not
> being with a letter from their master, or ticket, or not having a white
> person with them.[74]

However, these laws did not stop the slaves from communicating, from practicing their religion, from dancing, or from rebelling, for that matter. Instead of drums, they used their hands and feet to create sound and did not cross their feet when they danced. The Ring Shout endured primarily due to the importance of dancing and singing in praise of the ancestors and gods, but also because of its emphasis on clapping of hands instead of drumming and stamping of feet which did not cross. As Emery writes, "Since the Protestant church branded both the fiddle and the dance as sinful, and the drum had previously been banned due to its inflammatory nature, something had to be substituted."[75] Because they were not using drums and not "technically" dancing, the Ring Shout was not illegal and could be practiced more openly and more frequently than other traditions and thus had a better chance at surviving than the outlawed practices.

The Whitman Sisters' company repertory included Ballin' the Jack, a serpentine, circular, shuffling dance that had its roots in the plantation Ring Shout. No doubt the Whitmans learned some version of this dance when they were younger, as it was not completely banned by the church. In Ballin' the Jack, the head, shoulders and feet stay still while the rest of the body undulates and the hips rotate. A good description of the choreography comes from the lyrics to "Ballin' the Jack":

> First you put your two knees close tight
> Then you sway 'em to the left, then you sway 'em to the right
> Step around the floor kind of nice and light
> Then you twis' around and twis' around with all your might
> Stretch your lovin' arms straight out in space
> Then you do the Eagle Rock with style and grace
> Swing your foot way 'round then bring it back
> Now that's what I call "Ballin' the Jack."[76]

Similar to Ballin' the Jack was Snakehips, a hip gyration popularized by Earl Tucker. Animal dances like Snakehips, the Buzzard Lope, and the Fish Tail all had their roots in African dances.[77] Interestingly, very few critics actually describe the dance in detail, presumably for the sake of the reader's modesty. Contemporaries of Tucker, the Whitman Sisters' dancers performed their own version of Snakehips. Bennie Butler, a critic for the black newspaper *The Inter-State Tattler*, remarked on a Whitman Sisters Snakehips routine, "Three clever and charming young ladies register exceedingly well in a 'Snakehips' specialty that is a near show-stopper. Cute and vivacious, they imitate the gyrations of Mister Earl Tucker and I don't mean maybe."[78] These three youthful and charming dancers were usually Alice (the baby doll) and two other chorus members. Because they were "cute and vivacious," their movements would not be interpreted as risqué, and the company's moral standing could be preserved.

The Stearnses define one of the important characteristics of African dance as improvisation. "There is great emphasis placed on improvisation, often satirical, that allows for freedom of expression."[79] The spirit of improvisation in early black dance styles is captured in a description by Alice Whitman of a performance: "In Ballin' the Jack I'd stop in the middle of the song, squeal, and make my kneecaps quiver." When the bandleader asked her what she was doing, Alice responded, "I don't know what you call it but it sure feels good."[80] As Jacqui Malone reminds us, improvisation is a key element in creating and disseminating a vernacular dance.[81]

The Whitman Sisters also furthered other African American vernacular dance traditions by helping to popularize Walkin' the Dog, the Sand and the Shimmy, among others. For example, dressed as a man, Alberta did one of the first popular flash acts using such stunts as leaps, somersaults, and splits, and she claimed to have started the strut craze in black vernacular dance.[82]

The Whitman Sisters looked to African American performers who were already on the stage for examples of not only repertory but production and management strategies. A generation away from slavery, early African American performers could draw from only a very short, professional dramatic tradition within their own race. The significance of the Whitman Sisters' running their own company and making certain repertory choices becomes clearer when one realizes that very few companies prior to the Whitmans were black-owned and -managed. We can examine the choices made by these companies and individual black performers who predated the Whitman sisters in order to put them into proper context.

I have already discussed how the Whitman sisters worked from models established by the Fisk Jubilee Singers and the Hyer Sisters. Producer Bob Cole and the team of Williams and Walker also influenced the Whitman Sisters' work with their early versions of black musical comedy. Cole's *A Trip to Coontown* (1898) was the first all-Negro musical show conceived, directed, produced, and managed by African Americans. A show with a story line, it is credited with being the first "colored musical comedy."[83] Williams and Walker's "coon shows" laid the groundwork for images of African Americans on stage that resisted stereotypes.[84]

As I stated above, the earliest example of African American stage production, however, occurred in 1816, when Mr. Brown opened a tea garden in a thriving community of free African Americans in New York. This was the start of the first African American theater company—The African Grove Company—which featured some of the most renowned performers, such as James Hewlett and Ira Aldridge. The company produced at least three famous works. In *Tom and Jerry or Life in London,* they added a scene set in a slave market to evoke the antislavery sentiment of the audience, most of whom were among the few free people of African descent in the country. Their production of *Richard III* was also significant. By virtue of the fact that these were African American performers producing Shakespeare, they were harassed, arrested, and shut down several times. In retaliation for this treatment, Brown produced what may be seen as the first example of African American political protest theater. He wrote and produced *The Drama of King Shotaway*, the first play text known to have been written by an African American. This production, which occurred in the 1820s, some 40 years before the Civil War, portrayed a slave rebellion, included sympathetic slave characters, and depicted the leader of a slave rebellion as a hero.[85]

When the African Grove was finally shut down, neither Hewlett nor Aldridge was again able to perform in a play written by an African American, for an African American audience, with an African American company, managed by an African American. Aldridge did go on to perform in many Eurocentric roles, however, and when faced with the decision that many black performers at the time had to make—stay in the United States and be confined to minstrelsy, musical comedy, and dance, or move to Europe and be allowed more freedom to choose serious roles—Aldridge chose the latter. These and other racial tensions and strategies for resistance were a major part of the experiences of African American performers.[86]

❖ ❖ ❖

The Whitman Sisters also adopted styles from minstrel traditions. It is unfortunate that minstrelsy has the distinction of being labeled the first truly American theatrical art form, as it has done perhaps the most damage to the image of African Americans by perpetuating racist stereotypes. Minstrelsy is said to have begun when T. D. Rice, a white variety performer, encountered an old, crippled black man who was in the back alley of a theater before a performance in 1828. The man was doing a sort of jig and singing, "Wheel about and turn about and jump like so; and every time I turn about I jump Jim Crow." Fascinated by this performance, T. D. Rice bought the man's clothes, learned his little jig and introduced the character of Jim Crow that very night.[87] Although the origins of minstrelsy are apocryphal, the legacy of minstrelsy is clear: Jim Crow and other stock characters created for minstrelsy, including Mammy, Old Uncle, and Sambo, served as the central images of African Americans throughout the nineteenth century and reinforced degrading stereotypes that we are still fighting.

With the exception of William Henry Lane, known as Master Juba, who performed his jig dancing with several minstrel troupes in the 1840s, African Americans did not perform as minstrels until 1855, when Charles Hicks developed the Georgia Minstrels, the first all-black minstrel show. By 1865, "genuine" black minstrels were well established. They claimed to be more "authentic" than their white counterparts, many of whom had little or no connection to the Southern lifestyle they were purporting to re-create.[88] Thus, black male performers were able to start making a name for African Americans in popular entertainment. Unfortunately, they inherited the white-created stereotypes and, because most of their audiences were white, these performers had to fulfill white expectations and had little room to deviate from these detrimental images. In fact, as Robert Toll observes, many Northern audience members had never seen a slave and not only took minstrel portrayals as authentic, but actually mistook white minstrels in blackface for black people.[89] By watching minstrels, audience members were able to superficially and informally contend with race issues and form judgments about black identity.[90] When African Americans became minstrels, they had to darken their skin and widen their mouths. Some even took Irish names, because many white minstrels were Irish. This, as Leni Sloan claims, is an example of the "warping of the American fabric": Here were black men taking Irish names to impersonate the impersonator who impersonated them.[91] Or, as Brenda Dixon-Gottschild explains, "The intertexts of imitation-masking-disguising-displaying self as Other and Other as self are dense readings."[92] In the next chapter, I will analyze these negotiations further and detail how these intertexts operated within the Whitman sisters' work.

The ultimate irony was that the emergence of African American people in the theatrical workforce perpetuated degrading stereotypes of black people. Lawrence Levine, discussing the psychology of stereotypes, argues that when these images are persistently presented and reinforced, black people begin to be perceived as resembling them.[93] Although recognized as a grotesque genre and decried by black intellectuals at the time (especially philosopher Alain Locke and sociologist W. E. B. Du Bois) for sustaining stereotypes, minstrelsy and the practice of blacking up must nevertheless be understood as the first professional performance opportunity for African Americans, and its participants should be regarded as pioneers. For many black performers, minstrelsy was a way out of hunger, out of the Jim Crow South, and into adventure and other opportunities.[94]

Negro vaudeville was also influenced by several styles from Euro-American performance traditions. When different cultures are placed together, traditions are frequently transformed. This happened not only when different African ethnic groups labored side by side on the same plantation but also when people of African descent encountered Europeans, particularly the English and the Irish. The English traditions of music hall and variety shows had great bearing on all of American popular performance, and the Irish often lived in close proximity to African Americans in Northern cities.

English and Irish minstrels infused their own styles with steps some of them witnessed from African American performers to create new forms.[95] A clear example is the fusion of African steps with Irish jigs that resulted in an American (African American) tap dance tradition.[96]

The Whitman Sisters was perhaps best known for its tap dancing. Most of the famous tap dancers at the time were picks and, as stated earlier, the Whitman Sisters employed many picks, including Aaron Palmer, Samuel Reed, Julius Foxworth, and Tommy Hawkins. Albert "Pops" Whitman (son of Alice Whitman and Aaron Palmer) and Willie Robinson predated the acrobatic flash tap dancing of the Nicholas Brothers and the Berry Brothers by at least ten years with their own flash acts. Dancing the Charleston in a miniature tuxedo by the time he was four, Pops developed into one of the first great acrobatic tap dancers, a master of cartwheels, spins, flips, and splits. His partner Willie Robinson claims to have tutored the Nicholas brothers.[97] The group's shining star, however, was Alice, who was billed as "The Queen of Taps" and the best female tap dancer in the country[98]—quite an honor in this traditionally male line of business. Alice Whitman became one of the first nationally acclaimed black female tap dancers. Bennie Butler, critic for *The Inter-State Tattler,* called her "the china doll of syncopation, the peerless dancer, queen of them all."[99]

As stated above, the minstrel show was the most popular form of public amusement in the United States from the 1840s through the 1870s. The three-part minstrel structure consisted of a "walk around" in which performers in blackface stood in a semicircle singing and telling jokes. There was also a series of verbal exchanges between the end men, Tambo and Bones, and Mr. Interlocutor, who walked around in the center. The second section, or "olio," consisted of individual and smaller group acts, and the afterpiece was a short one-act skit, usually a plantation act that depicted the myth of the happy slaves. This structure greatly influenced vaudeville, and the Whitman Sisters' shows included not only individual and small group acts but a "befoh da wah" plantation skit as well.

Minstrelsy gave way to the rise of several forms of popular entertainment that gained momentum in the late nineteenth century. These diverse forms appealed to a wide variety of audience members of different classes and cultural backgrounds by offering lots of different styles at low prices. The more "legitimate" theater, on the other hand, targeted elite audiences.

The Whitman Sisters' repertory also built upon these Euro-American genres: extravaganza, burlesque, musical revue, and vaudeville.[100] The extravaganza theatrical form greatly influenced the direction of black vaudeville. This genre focused more on the spectacle of tableaux, costumes, scenic effects, dancing, and mime than on plot or character. Extravaganzas offered parodies of contemporary legitimate shows and popular stories. Music generally accompanied the improbable plots and spectacular presentations to make up an evening of light entertainment.

A subdivision of these extravaganzas was the burlesque. The popular burlesque shows of the 1870s through the 1920s were more raucous and bawdy than the earlier burlesque tradition, which satirized literature, theater and music. This middle form still drew from the comedy tropes of minstrelsy, adopting the same format, but included "leg" shows in which women would dance numbers that showed off their legs. Although the Whitman Sisters did not incorporate a later development in burlesque, strip tease, it did employ a number of chorus line women who were famous for dancing kicklines.

The musical revue was a topical variety show in which a group of performers presented several different skits. The revue premiered in 1894 in the United States with *The Passing Show* by George Lederer. At first, the musical revue was considered little more than glorified burlesque, but it became much more popular because it combined skits, songs, dance numbers, comic routines, and chorus girls. What made the musical revue different from other types of entertainment was the thematic coherence and acts that were created for a particular show. Although in the early years of the

Whitman Sisters the repertory consisted mostly of independent "turns," or acts, when the troupe joined Toby in the later years the shows were much more unified along particular themes. The Whitman Sisters never moved totally to the musical comedy genre, which was essentially a single play or narrative with interpolated songs and dances, but they did begin to move in that direction, with longer sketches and thematic consistency. There is no mention of performers with the Whitman Sisters playing consistent characters in an evening-length sketch with a single plot. The fact that they are always referred to as comics or singers or dancers suggests that the shows were closer to revues than musical comedies.

Tony Paster and B. F. Keith, two of the most influential white managers in show business at the time, were making significant improvements to the revue format by fusing together seemingly disparate elements of variety acts into what was to be called *vaudeville*. English variety and music hall shows attempted to provide audiences with multiple styles of performance in order to appeal to many different tastes. The French also had a pastoral play with musical interludes that influenced American vaudeville. Vaudeville combined variety acts that were carefully constructed along standard formulas but without connective plots. These familiar formulas provided rhythm, pace, and a sense of unity. A typical show offered a taste of many different styles in 8 to 14 turns consisting of musical numbers (especially solo and duo vocals), dance numbers, combination song and dance acts, comic routines, and sometimes magic acts, acrobatics, juggling, and animal acts.

Vaudeville entrepreneurs attempted to promote their genre as more respectable than other forms of popular entertainment. In order to foster this respectable image, they named many of the vaudeville houses "music halls," "academies" and "museums with lecture halls," rather than use the less respectable word "theater."[101] Big-time vaudeville consisted of the major theaters in large urban areas that offered twice-a-day straight vaudeville (without films). This was the upper echelon of show business, and the pinnacle of big-time was the Palace Theater in New York City. Small-time, in contrast, usually consisted of theaters in small cities that played bills continuously, three or more times a day. Big-time performers were obviously paid more and generally treated better than "small-timers."

The overarching goal of vaudeville, with its smorgasbord of material, was to appeal to a wide variety of spectators. There was supposed to be something for everyone; if one turn failed to entertain a person, the next would. Conspicuously absent from the artistic formulation of these objectives are the African American spectator and performer. For the most part barred from vaudeville, African American performers like the Whitman

Sisters took it upon themselves to create their own style within this genre. Black vaudevillians built upon these traditions to create entertainment that offered something for every black audience member. These performers had relatively steady and well-paid work and were given the freedom to create anything that would attract a paying audience.[102] They also offered a different voice in the entertainment industry, making innovations within these styles and starting new traditions.

From this brief discussion, we can see that at the disposal of African American performers from many different traditions, black and white, was a vast repertory of material. Black vaudevillians assembled these multiple traditions into a performance genre that allowed them to capitalize on, critique, and reinvent the entertainment industry. The Whitman sisters drew from all of these traditions in order to create their shows. However, as I discuss later, it was the African American traditions and community to which the Whitman Sisters were particularly dedicated. In 1898 writer/producer Bob Cole issued his Colored Actors' Declaration of Independence, a sentiment later echoed by W. E. B. Du Bois in the 1920s and the revolutionary playwright Amiri Baraka in the 1960s. Cole said: "We are going to have our own shows. We are going to write them ourselves, we are going to have our own stage managers, our own orchestra leader and our own manager out front to count up. No divided houses—our race must be seated from the boxes back."[103] By preserving, improving, and perpetuating their heritage, the Whitman Sisters more than succeeded in this endeavor. They thrived.

"THEY ARE THE GREATEST GENIUSES UPON THE STAGE":[104] A RECONSTRUCTION OF A TYPICAL WHITMAN PERFORMANCE

The above discussion of the Whitman Sisters' influences and the theatrical world in which they prospered helps us put the following reconstruction into context. Below, I have compiled accounts from the sisters and others who performed with them to produce a reconstruction of a typical performance by the Whitman Sisters during the high point of the early years from 1909 to 1920. Although I speculate on the order in which some of the acts appeared, based on knowledge of theatrical traditions and the practices of contemporaneous black vaudeville performers,[105] I do not speculate when I describe an act. All of the descriptions are taken from accounts of events that took place.[106] We know that the company performed both in theaters and in churches. Although nowhere in the source materials does anyone make reference to changing the repertory for a church audience, the Whitman Sisters were careful about promoting the upstanding image for the company, so one might assume that some movements and some jokes presented in a theater might not have been repeated in the sisters' church shows. For example, in an interview Alice talks about dancing on stage wearing a short skirt and swinging her hips around suggestively.[107] For a church audience the costume may have been lengthened and the movement might have been toned down or cut altogether.

The goal of this reconstruction is to give the reader a better sense of what a Whitman Sisters show was like. I will defer an analysis of issues arising from performance to the following chapters.

The Whitman Sisters offered something for everyone: jubilee songs and coon shouts, cakewalks and breakdowns, comedians, midgets, cross-dressers, beautiful dancing girls, pickaninnies, a jazz band, and, after their invention in the 1920s, talkies.

No matter the weather, crowds packed into the standing-room-only local theater house, or perhaps a black church set up to accommodate theatrics, to see the Whitman Sisters revue.[108] Patrons who could not get in waited outside to catch a glimpse of the show or to hear some of the songs. The reviews in the paper were raves, as usual.[109] All of the most distinguished members of the African American community, including professionals and the clergy, went to see the Whitman sisters, who for a few weeks at a time would take a city by storm.

Several hours before the audience arrived, Mabel was probably arguing with the theater manager, who was trying to cheat the company, most likely attempting to pay the company less than the agreed-upon salary. Mabel would threaten to pull the show at the last minute, and when the manager called her bluff, he would find that she was not bluffing. He probably would give in and return to the original price, but this time Mabel would demand full payment in advance to ensure that he did not cheat the company.[110] She had won.

Mabel's next duty was to oversee the final rehearsal. Seeking perfection, she would yell at the dancers, "Get those feet *up* there. What the hell do you think you're doing? Get those feet moving!"[111] During the course of this final rehearsal, she would probably make some last-minute repertory changes if any of the acts was not to her liking.

After the final dress, about 25 performers would scramble to get into costumes and makeup. Dancers would stretch out and singers would warm up their voices while Essie fixed the stitching on costumes. Mabel would decide upon which of the eight different programs the company would perform that night, inform the performers of the order and give notes to iron out rough spots in the numbers. She might tell one of the picks that his act would be cut in half because he had not perfected his moves or because he was upstaging too many other performers. The little boy would probably cry but could not fathom leaving the show and going home because everyone knew that "[w]hen you joined the Whitman Sisters, you went with them, you worked with them, and you just learned—that was all. You just learned to perform."[112] This was the best show business education around and for a pick with the Whitmans, "[y]ou sang one week, danced the next, sold peanuts the next, and if you got caught breaking any of the rules they shipped you home in a hurry."[113]

Upon entering the theater, white and black patrons may have expected the usual segregation pattern, with whites in the auditorium and blacks in the balcony, which was known as "Nigger Heaven." However, the Whitmans refused to play to houses segregated in this way, and insisted upon blacks being allowed in the parquet and dress circle sections of the theater.[114] Although theatergoers were probably still grouped together by race, the Whitman sisters' first attempts at desegregation were important ones, as I will argue later.

The eight-member jazz band, led by Bennie Moten[115] and featuring the young Bill (who later added "Count" to his stage name) Basie, would play an overture, either an old favorite or a new piece written for the show by Alberta or Moten, perhaps offering a taste of the music they would play between each act. Mabel would be the first to walk onto stage, and when the applause died down she would tell of the sisters' childhood, about how they had taken a prominent part in church activities as well as concert work, because their father was a minister of the gospel. She would go on to tell about their tutelage under their father, their hometown elementary school education, the New England Conservatory of Music and Morris Brown

College in Atlanta where they seriously studied music. She would describe their first concert and briefly tell the history of how they came by their success.[116] When she finished her oration, the band would play an upbeat popular number to warm the audience up and then switch to a sentimental sorrow song such as "Who Dat Comin' Ovah Yondah?"[117] which was undoubtedly well known to all there. The curtain would rise to reveal a "befoh da wah" plantation act, reminiscent of minstrel shows. Mammy (probably Mabel) would be in blackface makeup peeling potatoes and the picks would be singing and dancing around her, also perhaps in blackface, in the quaint setting of a Southern cottage dooryard at eventide.[118]

The backdrop was probably a painted scene with painted flats on either side that could easily be switched between the acts. Lighting likely consisted of basic lights (on and off), although minimal effects may have been used to achieve an evening atmosphere, as gas lighting instruments were becoming more widely used and afforded more creative lighting solutions.

Mammy's son, usually played by Willie Robinson, a.k.a. the "Little Georgia Blossom," would return home with a rooster for supper, thereby prompting Mammy to praise the Lord by singing psalms.[119]

Next would come the specialty numbers, solo singers and dancers. Willie Toosweet and "Sparkplug" George would perform a comedy act punctuated by Sparkplug's famous foghorn laugh, a laugh that inspired one critic to remark, "When he's all washed up as a comedian, he should visit the tug-boat lines along the Hudson River and get a job, laughing in a fog."[120] The young Ethel Waters would then come out and do her famous coon shouting, a vocal technique that emphasized both sacred shouting and moans, blues, and ballads. Shouters like Waters, Clara Smith (known as the "World's Greatest Moaner"), and Bessie Love could put over a song and shout about anything, easily singing both sharp and flat, with many voice breaks.

Pops Whitman or Willie Robinson would probably be featured next singing popular songs such as "Is Everybody Happy?" while they nimbly danced breakdowns.[121] Robinson, who was "as big as a couple of bunches of toothpicks," had a sense of humor that would "make a cow smile."[122] Essie Whitman would follow with a drunk act that presented the audience with the character of "The Beggar" who delighted all with comedic elocution.[123]

Then would come the dancers! They had the stage to themselves and did not have to sing or tell jokes as in the prior tent show tradition, but were able to dance as a sole specialty.[124] They would probably prance onto stage with a cakewalk and then move into a Tiller dance, a popular, intricate combination of high kicking on alternating legs in a typical chorus line fashion. As Catherine Basie (wife of Bill) described, they would "kick to the left, kick to the right, kick straight up, and so on, to the tune of the jazzy 'Stardust.'"[125] Then three of the girls—Alice Whitman, Jeni LeGon, and Catherine Basie—would do a shake dance (something like the Shimmy) to the jazz song "Diga Diga Doo." Shifting focus to the lower half of the body, the girls would then do a Snakehips dance that rivaled the one performed by the original "Snake Hips" Tucker himself. They would wear shimmering orange blouses with big sleeves, green satin pants and sashes around their waists. Because of the movement of the satin, when they would shake and snake, it *all* shook and all of the undulations up and down the body were emphasized. This was a show stopper in theaters though it was probably tamed down in church performances.[126]

After perhaps a solo by a singer, probably a newcomer who could not complain about having to follow such a crowd pleaser, the three-foot-tall singing comedienne Princess Wee Wee, and six-foot-tall, teenaged Willie Bryant would pair up to sing, dance, and tell jokes in an act that kept audiences doubled over in laughter. The public at this time was still enthralled with the bizarre pseudo-scientific exhibits of shows like P. T. Barnum's circuses, which included the African American performers Jo-Jo the Dogface Boy, Zip the Pin-Headed Man, Millie and Christina the Siamese Twins, and numerous fat ladies.[127] Capitalizing on this trend, the Whitman Sisters hired the yard-high Princess Wee Wee and featured her as a marvel of nature. The sisters had discovered the talented midget and adopted her, and she became one of the chief attractions of the show. The top of her head reached Bryant's waist when they danced their duet. She was billed as "the world's smallest perfect woman," "the most talented midget in the world" and "the smallest Racial performer on the American stage."[128] "She'd sing in a cute, high-pitched voice," said Bryant, "and then she'd dance around and between my legs."[129] Ernestine Lucas talks about seeing Princess Wee Wee perform and being awestruck by not only her size but her "air of dignity" as well.[130]

Mabel may have then performed again with her picks.[131] She would sing some of the old favorites and then turn the show over to the boys, who would wow the audiences with their unstoppable energy—belting out songs, clapping out a Charleston rhythm, tapping like there was no tomorrow, turning flips, running up walls, and generally defying gravity and most other laws of physics. They probably also sang "coon songs," vestiges of minstrelsy that entertained but perpetuated black stereotypes including fried chicken eating, fancy clothes, and rowdiness. According to the Stearnses, picks were so popular that the head of a vaudeville circuit once said: "If the bill is weak, add a Negro act, and if that don't do it, hire some Negro kids."[132]

Paul Laurence Dunbar's lyrics for *Clorindy* illustrate the type of songs the picks would have sung:

> Who dat say chicken in dis crowd?
> Speak de word agin' and speak it loud
> Blame de lan' let white folk rule it,
> I'se a lookin' fuh a pullet
> Who dat say chicken in dis crowd?

or

> Behold the hottest coon,
> Your eyes e'er lit on,
> Velvet ain't good enough,
> For him to sit on,
> When he goes to town
> Folks yell like sixty,
> Behold the hottest coon in Dixie.[133]

Butterbeans and Susie (Jodie Edwards and Susie Edwards) perfected their husband and wife skits and characters while with the Whitman Sisters. The henpecked husband and nagging wife, on the order of Kingfish and Sapphire from the *Amos 'n' Andy* radio shows in the late 1920s and television series of the 1950s and Ralph and Alice from the 1950s television series *The Honeymooners*, told low jokes, danced, heckled, and insulted each other.[134] Butterbeans tried to stand up to his domineering wife, but his small stature and less than imposing physicality only increased the hilarity of the situation. Susie sang the blues and cakewalked, and Butterbeans performed the Itch, also known as the Heebie Jeebies, in which he scratched himself in syncopation.[135]

When Butterbeans and Susie had finished their repartee, a handsome and debonair gentleman would then strut upon the stage, the epitome of class and style. Baby doll Alice Whitman would do a series of shuffles (skipping steps that resulted in two tap sounds for each step) to get onto the stage; cute as a button, she and the man would dance a duet while a chorus line came on as backup. At different points during the act, spectators would realize that the man was actually a woman, none other than Alberta Whitman, a.k.a. Bert, the famous male impersonator. Willie Bryant would then come out and make it into a trio dance, somewhat like the famous dance team of Bert Williams, George Walker, and Ada Overton

Walker. Alice would then begin to sing her number and the stage would clear as she broke into a clear, clean tap routine full of wings, pullbacks, and time steps that put most tappers to shame. Still in her baby doll costume (see Figure 3), Alice exuded dainty charm. As she is pictured here with her oversized bows, head tilted in innocence, and childlike expression, she is the epitome of purity.

The star of the show, Alice did Ballin' the Jack, Walkin' the Dog, the Sand, and the Shimmy. The Stearnses go on to describe her act:

> When the chorus line went off before her specialty, Alice sang with a voice something like Helen Kane's [a 1920s songstress noted for having a particularly sexy voice].

"I'd make my exit with the Shim-Sham-Shimmy [a dance step isolating various parts of the body in a side-to-side motion], mostly from the waist down—along with more squeals—wearing a shawl and a little flimsy thing around my middle with a fringe and a bow on the back. If I ever lost that bow, they used to say, I'd sure catch cold . . . I could swing a mean [Alice winked her eye] around."[136]

Alice's reputation for tapping was well known. According to Buster Brown "Oh, Pops' mother was a great dancer. Her name was Alice Whitman and she was a wonderful dancer."[137] Jeni LeGon stated:

> Of the tap dancers (Alice) was the best there was. She was tops. She was better than Ann Miller and Eleanor Powell and me and anybody else you wanted to put her to. . . . She could do all the ballet-style stuff like Eleanor. And then she could hoof [heavy, grounded tapping]! But she never went out on her own, you know, she stayed with the sisters.[138]

Alice often had to "vamp," or repeat two to four measures of her number several times, as Essie took a long time backstage getting her appearance just right. "I'd take a dozen encores waiting for Sister Essie to make that one spit curl backstage. 'Fess' would be going 'Doo-dee-doo-dee-doo' on the piano, vamping for her, until she finally came out."[139] Finally Essie would reappear, this time not as a character, but as a serious singer, amazing audiences with her rendition of "Some of These Days" in a contralto that reputedly made the famous low-range singer Sophie Tucker sound like a soprano. Essie's stage personae was very similar to Mae West and has led to questions about who influenced whom.

Figure 3. Alice Whitman. Reproduced courtesy of the Billy Rose Theatre Collection,
The New York Public Library for the Performing Arts.
Astor, Lenox, and Tilden Foundations.

After a short intermission, perhaps, four women with blonde hair in "Gibson girl" style would then appear, parade around the stage and sing a few songs.[140] Spectators may or may not have recognized them as the Whitman sisters themselves. A blues singer and possibly a comedy act followed. Mabel then did her solo act (see Figure 4), and Alberta began the finale with a strut and what was known as flash dancing or legomania, throwing her legs every which way.[141] The finale was a huge production number, with every member of the company perhaps taking a turn, leaving the audience with a memory of the best parts of their acts. The entire company would do a Cakewalk and end in a spectacular group kickline, feeding off the audience's applause, intensifying the electricity in the air as the curtain came down on the seemingly never-ending vitality of spirited singing and dancing. As an encore, Pops would come out and dance one last number to close the show.

After the audience left, Mabel would bring the cast out onto the stage and give her lecture or, as some called it, her sermon.[142] She gave notes on the night's performances: perhaps the show ran longer than the usual hour and fifteen minutes, or a technical element did not happen on cue. She would tell all the children that they had to finish their schoolwork the next day for their tutor, her husband, Dave Payton, or they would not be allowed to perform in the next show. She played the roles of preacher, director, and mother as she morally admonished the cast, walking back and forth chewing gum and "putting the fear of hell-fire and brimstone into her protégés. . . . Mabel had a stentorian voice and a powerful frown. . . . She looked like a stern school principal."[143] If this were the last show on the second Thursday night, the company would then pack up and prepare to move to the next town. Mabel would say something like:

> Now when we get to Cuthbert, the married couples will live together and the unmarried couples will not. It's a mortal sin, and I don't want to catch any of you young girls staying with any boys. Is that clear?[144]

With Mabel's final reproaching words, the company would pack up and head to the next town, which was eagerly awaiting its arrival.

Figure 5 shows the company and band with 26 members in 1928. Other musicians shown are part of the Doc Hyder Orchestra.

Figure 4. Mabel Whitman. Reproduced courtesy of the Billy Rose Theatre Collection, The New York Public Library for the Performing Arts. Astor, Lenox, and Tilden Foundations.

Figure 5. The Whitman Sisters Company 1928. Some band members are part of the Doc Hyder Orchestra, the others are part of the Whitman Sisters band. Photo taken at the Dunbar Theatre, Philadelphia, December 1928. Pictured from left to right are: Marbel Wilson—chorus girl, Charlie Anderson—singer, yodeler, Leo Watson—singer, Alex Stevens—trumpet (Doc Hyder), Alfreda Allman—dancer, Bernard Archer—trombone (Doc Hyder), ? Mason—trumpet (Whitman Sisters), Clyde Bernhardt—trombone (Whitman Sisters), Delores Payne—chorus girl, ?—trumpet (Doc Hyder), Myrtle Fortune—chorus girl, Sambo Reed—comedian, ?—tuba (Doc Hyder), Troy Snapp—piano leader (Whitman Sisters), Billie Yates—of Pops and Billie duo (Whitman Sisters), Ellis Reynolds—piano (Doc Hyder), Doc Hyder—band leader (Doc Hyder), Princess Wee Wee—dancer, Leslie Towels—drums (Whitman Sisters), Alice Whitman—tap dancer, ?—drums (Doc Hyder), Albert "Pops" Whitman—dancer, Alberta "Bert" Whitman—male impersonator, Willie Too Sweet—comedian, ?—banjo (Doc Hyder), Bernice Ellis—leading lady, Katie Franklin—chorus girl, Sterling Payne—alto sax (Whitman Sisters), Josh Saddler—violin (Doc Hyder), Ethel Frye—chorus girl, ?—alto sax (Doc Hyder), Archie Anderson—violin (Whitman Sisters), Douglas Daniels—?, ?—clarinet (Whitman Sisters), ?—tenor sax (Doc Hyder), Margaret Watkins—soubrette, ?—alto sax (Doc Hyder), Hubert ?—singer, straight man. Reproduced courtesy of the Frank Diggs Collection-Archive Photos.

Race, Gender, and Class: The Politics of Performance and Management

IN THIS CHAPTER I ANALYZE all of the primary and secondary materials on the Whitman Sisters in order to draw conclusions about how they functioned in and transformed the theater world they encountered. The chapter is divided into three sections. In the first I analyze the race and gender politics the company faced on stage. Several theories help me analyze how the company operated as a black company run by light-complexioned black women[1] who at times performed in blackface, re-created potentially damaging minstrel images, passed for white on and off stage, refused to perpetuate light-skinned beauty standards, and challenged repertory norms by presenting women in traditionally male roles, capitalizing on sexuality and cross-dressing. The theories I use include semiotics, theories of the body in representation and construction (especially Foucault), gaze theory, and signifying. These refigurings of race and gender were possible in part because the sisters maintained a "high-class" image for themselves and their company.

In the second section of this chapter, I analyze the Whitman Sisters' class negotiations and discuss the ways in which these figured with race and gender. In particular, I interrogate how class interactions, respectability, and theories of racial uplift played important roles in the Whitman Sisters' development as a major vaudeville company. I also examine how class functioned theoretically in terms of the body. By placing the Whitman Sisters in the context of the African American class structure at the beginning of the twentieth century, I am able to draw conclusions about the importance of the concepts of uplift, true womanhood, and double consciousness for the Whitman Sisters in their public life, their interactions in the theater, and their relationship to the African American community. Not only were negotiations of race, gender, and class important to the Whitman Sisters' repertory, and social interactions, they were also vital to the business dealings of the company.

In the third section of this chapter, I analyze the race, gender, and class politics of the company's offstage dealings and detail their unlikely recipe for success. I place into context Mabel's role as a black female manager at this time. I discuss how she dealt with white competition, racism, and sexism. I also show how Mabel used race, gender, and class to her advantage in garnering talent and securing bookings and how she fought for and protected the rights of African American patrons and performers.

WHAT ARE THOSE WHITE WOMEN DOING UP THERE?: IDENTITY POLITICS AND THE NEGOTIATION OF RACE AND GENDER

On and off stage, the Whitman sisters masterfully negotiated and renegotiated the ways in which they were perceived in terms of race and gender.[2] They passed for white on and off stage; Mabel altered some of the images of minstrelsy, and Alberta was a skilled cross-dresser. These acts were significant, not just in the ways they entertained audiences, but also in the ways they commented on society. In this section, I show that, in these situations, the Whitman sisters shared in the power dynamics at work and the production of meaning. Rather than remain powerless objects, passive to the spectator's gaze, the Whitman sisters, as I will show, took agency over their images and resisted accepted representations.

Perhaps a playgoer who walked into a Whitman Sisters show expected to be entertained by four black women and their company of performers. What happened when he or she was presented instead with the absolute disruption of these expectations? A boy/girl team danced a duet and sometime in the midst of it the spectator realized that the man was a woman. Four white women appeared in full Gibson Girl style with high blonde pompadours. The audience member must have double-checked the program thinking he or she was in the wrong theater.

Aware of the politics of performance and representation, the sisters formulated several identities or personas for themselves in order to entertain. In the process they shocked, confronted, and challenged their audiences to recognize the tenuousness of rigid constructions of race and gender. As Judith Butler articulates, identity is not fixed, but rather made manifest through power relations and is performative, meaning a "regularized and constrained repetition of norms."[3]

> Performance is not a singular act or event, but a ritualized production, a ritual reiterated under and through constraint, under and through the force of prohibition and taboo, with the threat of ostracism and even death controlling and compelling the shape of the production, but not, I will insist, determining it fully in advance.[4]

Although by law African Americans at the turn of the century were denied access to most public spaces, including restaurants, parks, and many theaters, the spaces to which they were permitted access, such as a handful of theaters, served as interstitial sites where confrontations between binaries (black/white, male/female, etc.) could take place.[5] Performers crossed the liminal space of theaters and were able to safely try on different identities and experiment with, rework, and resignify seeming norms.

As I will show, by disrupting the repetition of norms, the Whitman Sisters called attention to the power relations at work. Performers such as the Whitman Sisters took agency over their images and experimented with a constantly shifting, fluid portrayal of self. They refused to accept the standard, singular definition of what black women were supposed to do, how they were supposed to look, and where they were supposed to work.

How do we know a black woman when we see one? By the color of her skin, by the percentage of black blood given her by her ancestors, by the shape of her body, by the way she walks, by the way she talks? We have learned to read the signs, and we don't consider recognition a complex task but rather assume that it is instinctive, effortless, natural. Identifying a black woman often takes us no longer than a fraction of a second, and our certainty is close to 100 percent. But what happens when the signs we have learned to read no longer signify the expected? What happens when recognizing a black woman as a black woman takes a few minutes instead of a few milliseconds? The obvious becomes less dependable, and we must convince ourselves of her identity. The very certainty of a sexed, raced being becomes compromised and the categories by which identity of the Other is defined are challenged.

In order to analyze the sisters' repertory choices and to draw conclusions about how audiences experienced the Whitman Sisters, we need a semiotics of the body and a discourse of identity. In other words, we need a way of "reading" their physical performances and understanding their implications on notions of self and society. Understanding that the body is a project of signification with identity as the referent, we need to decode this project in order to comprehend the complex negotiations at work in performance. Analytic theory that examines implications of the performing body allows us to understand the control performers exercise over their bodies and the consequences for theories of the "natural" or "essential body."

Semiotics provides us with valuable analytical tools for analyzing representation of the body in the Whitman Sisters' performances in terms of race and gender. Using semiotics, feminists in particular have made many advancements in analyzing signification on the stage.[6] Primarily focused on gender, these theorists often neglect race. However, when these theories are combined with an analysis of race, they are valuable for understanding the Whitman Sisters' work. Iconic symbols, or signs/signifiers, convey a meaning that is "read" in light of a particular referent as well as a culturally defined metaphorical representation. In theater, these signs are infused with meaning—in other words, encoded. These images are potentially read differently by different audience members based on their own sense of racial and gender identity. The image of a black female body on stage engaged in a particular act is inscribed with a certain significance different from that of any other body.

Central to this reading of the body is the issue of representation. How is the body presented or represented? How is it read? What are the broader implications? Just about everything on the stage is a representation, but by decoding the signs according to theories of signification and semiotics, we are able to better understand the performers, the audience, the presentation and the significance.

In the United States, black female performers have always had to wage a battle for power over representation. Playing with or against the expected, often stereotyped characterizations permitted them, these women had to find ways to balance power so that they could both entertain and maintain their dignity. Some of these women played into stereotypes because the real financial benefits and the limited career alternatives available to them outweighed all other considerations. For example, Hattie McDaniel, who perfected the role of Mammy in the 1930s, was once asked whether she thought it was degrading to play maids all of the time. She said, "I can play a maid for $700 a week or I can be a maid for $7 a week."[7] Others, like the Whitman Sisters, found ways to gain more control over their bodies and representations, while remaining economically successful and popular.

In *The Body and Social Theory*, Chris Shilling argues that in the late twentieth century, the body is becoming a phenomenon of options and choices as a result of developments such as biological reproduction, genetic engineering, plastic surgery, and sports science.[8] However, as we see with the Whitman Sisters, the idea of the body as a phenomenon of options was at work in the early twentieth century as well. Although the technologies of plastic surgery or the like were not available, theater conventions allowed performers to alter their appearances. Later work on how the body is construed and operates socially therefore can help us decode the work of these performers. As opposed to an essentialist position that would argue that identity is solely predetermined by biology and is static despite social forces, my work is based on the understanding of the raced and sexed body as a social construct and identity as determined by external and internal forces.[9] Even at the beginning of the twentieth century, choices about representation greatly affected how one was identified and challenged notions of a fixed identity. Both the individual and society help shape identity. And no matter the individually determined identity, social forces converge to determine how the individual is seen by others, judged, and overall, identified. "The body vanishes as a biological entity and becomes a socially constructed product which is infinitely malleable and highly unstable."[10] As Omi and Winant similarly discuss,

> Thus race, class, and gender (as well as sexual orientation) constitute "regions" of hegemony, areas in which certain political projects can take shape. They share certain obvious attributes in that they are all "socially constructed," and they all consist of a field of projects whose common feature is their linkage of social structure and signification.[11]

These constructions are ongoing projects. When social forces change with shifts in racism, sexism, or classism, so do the constructions of identity as they are read on the body.

Foucault's theories on the body are also very useful for explaining the identity politics surrounding the Whitman Sisters performances.[12] Foucault describes the social forces that discipline bodies in order to exercise power over lives.[13] Bodies are forced to conform to discipline and to standards that contemporaneous society demands. This pliant Foucaultian discursive body can be invested with various and changing forms of power that alternately control and are controlled by individuals and society. For example, the watcher has the power to define the watched body and thereby control it, while the one being watched is relegated to object status and is ever self-consciously mindful of the power of the look. The subject is always the potential object of the gaze and thereby internalizes the gaze. We see this with the Panopticon, the prison with a tower in the center that allows the inmate to be seen at all times; because the tower is dark to the inmate, she never knows when she is being watched or by whom specifically. The inmate is in a state of conscious and permanent visibility as she knows she may always be watched. Thus "visibility is a trap."[14] With this example, we see how the gaze induces self-monitoring as a method of social control. This is crucial to understanding the discursive networks of power. In the Panopticon, the watched cannot watch and therefore has no control over the surveillance.

However, I argue that in other social relationships, especially the performer/spectator dynamic for the purposes of our discussion, the watcher and the watched can share the power in determining identity. These perceptions may not necessarily coincide, and the balance of power may be fluid and shifting, but both parties participate in the identification. As meanings are determined by a shared vocabulary of body idiom and social forces and attributed to the body, the body as we know it is thereby produced. Jill Dolan argues that gender "becomes a social gestus, a gesture that represents ideology circulating in social relations."[15] I would extend this argument to include race. In other words, by analyzing the ways in which race and gender are perceived on stage, we can say much about social relations. Bodies, on which the gestus is read, become what Gillian Rose calls "maps of the relation between power and identity."[16] By reading these maps, by reading the body, we can draw conclusions about social power, gaze theory, semiotics and theories of the body.

These theories investigate the ways the body is perceived in everyday life and challenge the relationship between representation and identity. On the stage, the body has always been considered a site of possibilities. Audiences are willing to suspend disbelief, imagine, and accept the projection as real, at least for a moment. The body is shapeable, and the performer molds it into characters to perpetuate the illusion.

Different spectators respond differently to performances. In the case of the Whitman Sisters, a white man may have had a reaction to the sisters' passing for white very different from that of a black woman; some audience members would have suspended their disbelief more than others. We can, nonetheless, draw conclusions about the impact the Whitman Sisters had on its audiences and the ways in which expectations were challenged based on written responses and theater conventions at this time.

The body on stage can also be understood in terms of the economics of commodification. The spectator pays to witness this altered body, and there exists a real exchange of cash for services. Perhaps the most important question is, Who has the power: the watcher or the watched? Who can ultimately define the "actual" body? Do performers control their representation because it is they who don the costumes, speak the lines, and move across stage as the spectator passively absorbs the representation? Or rather, does the spectator have the power to interpret and define the reality of the experience no matter what the performer intends? As I stated above, many gaze theorists asked this question and concluded that the watcher possesses the power to define while the watched is reduced to object status. Examining the Whitman Sisters, however, we find different dynamics in operation.

An examination using gaze theory, as discussed mainly by feminist film theorists, modified with other theories to accommodate race, helps us understand the dynamics in operation between the observer at a Whitman Sisters' show and the performer. Although feminist film theory examines the camera as a medium, we can use this work, nonetheless, to examine the power dynamics at work in a live performance.[17] Instead of the camera directing the audience's gaze, a spectator in the theater can direct her or his own gaze, to some extent, within the confines of the stage. Without anachronistically attributing feminist or modern racially aware sensibilities to the Whitman Sisters' audiences, I want to argue that the performers' "play" on race and gender identity could be read as cultural commentary and that audiences picked up on (to different degrees, consciously or subconsciously) the significance of race and gender bending in the Whitman Sisters' performances.

We learn from this branch of feminist theory that *gender* can be defined as the individual's relationship to his or her sex, which is a biological demarcation based on genital paraphernalia. This relationship is influenced by not only personal choices, but also societal forces. According to Laura Mulvey and other gaze theorists, a spectator's way of looking is necessarily gender marked. I will argue that it is also racially marked based on the individual's relationship to his or her color, nationality, and history.

The ground-laying arguments of gaze theory made by theorists such as Laura Mulvey and Teresa de Lauretis claim that a male heterosexual spectatorship controls narratives, objectifies women, and is assumed in American performances throughout history. Mulvey claims that the female image is constructed by men to be viewed by other men as an object. "In a world ordered by sexual imbalance, pleasure in looking has been split between active/male and passive/female. The determining male gaze projects its fantasy onto the female figure, which is styled accordingly."[18] The female appearance is coded to produce an erotic impact so that women connote what Mulvey calls "to-be-looked-at-ness."[19] The female spectator is in a problematic position because she is unable to "look" because the economy of the gaze is male.[20] Mulvey, therefore, calls for a freeing of the look of the audience into dialectics with passionate detachment.[21]

These gaze theories are important for evaluating the ways in which sexual politics and performance interact. However, they are insufficient for analyzing the works of a group such as the Whitman Sisters. When analyzing the company, we must move beyond this model to one that allows for the possibility of multiple spectatorships within a single performance and potential shifts in the power of looking.[22] The Whitman sisters assumed a mixed audience in terms of gender and race; indeed they actively fought for desegregated audiences and had performances deemed "respectable enough" for women.[23] Also, it was not the case that men were creating images of women for other men. Instead, the sisters ran every aspect of the show and thus we have an example of women in the position of presenting images to an audience where male, female, black, and white can look.

Therefore, we require a more complex theoretical reading of the race and gender politics and concepts of looking than we get with traditional gaze theory. Several additional theories help us complete the picture.

The reinvention of self and the manipulation of images were not new concepts to early African American performers. Gottschild traces this tradition to African sources: "African peoples are well-versed in the art of role playing and role reversal, concealing and revealing, double entendre and innuendo. These are positive characteristics and basic integers in the Africanist aesthetic."[24] Using Henry Louis Gates's theories, we can see this practice as part of the tradition of "signifyin'," or repetition with a critical change or a signal difference. In his work on African American literary criticism, [25] Gates proposes a theory for understanding black vernacular discourse that is double voiced and obscures apparent meaning. The black rhetorical tropes include marking, loud talking, testifying, calling out (of one's name), sounding, rapping, and "playing the dozens."[26] For example, in *The Signifying Monkey* poems, the trickster monkey confronts the lion and uses the technique of indirect argument or persuasion and implies, begs, goads, or boasts by indirect verbal or gestural means. In this manner the monkey gets his way with the lion. Although Gates is primarily concerned with language and the production of meaning in literary narratives, his theories can be extended to include an analysis of the performative, or gesture, and the production of meaning. As Sandra L. Richards argues in "Writing the Absent Potential: Drama, Performance, and the Canon of African American Literature,"

> The critical tradition within African American literature locates "authentic" cultural expression on the terrain of the folk, but the folk have articulated their presence most brilliantly in those realms with which literature is uncomfortable, namely in arenas centered in performance.[27]

As such, expanding African American literary criticism to the performative is a logical step, especially in terms of the power of narrative to alter meaning.

We can further link theories on the vernacular with the performative if we look at the work of Judith Butler on performativity alongside Gates's literary theory. As Butler articulates, "There is power and agency in repeating restrictive hegemonic terms/norms in directions that reverse, displace, critique their originating aims."[28] When a symbolic gesture or utterance is revised, critiqued, or parodied, new meanings are created echoing the past and foreshadowing the future. Gates similarly writes: "Writers signify upon each other's texts by rewriting the received textual tradition. . . . This sort of Signifyin(g) revision serves, if successful, to create a space for the revising text. It also alters fundamentally the way we read the tradition."[29] In theater, we have the example of this type of revision when we look at black minstrels who made small but significant changes in minstrelsy when they took over the formats created by their white counterparts. While maintaining a claim to authenticity, they altered certain themes to criticize the idealized image of the South that glorified a fictional plantation life replete with content slaves and benevolent masters. For example, white minstrels created Old Darky to be a sentimental, nostalgic character who loved his white master and mistress and wouldn't take his freedom if it were handed to him. Black minstrels kept the sentimentality of Old Darky, but in their manifestations he now longed for his wife and children sold away from him by a much crueler master and mistress. Black minstrels were thus able to incorporate resistance as an undercurrent and developed masks that satisfied white expectations while subverting negative images and creating a hidden culture.

Also, as I mention above, in dance, the Cakewalk developed as a pastiche of the dances slaves witnessed their white masters and mistresses performing in the Big House. Certain meanings were encoded and although apparent to those in the know (the slaves), were read differently by the white people who had the slaves perform this dance for them. For these spectators, the Cakewalk was an amusing attempt at sophistication on the parts of their slaves, rather than a mockery of their lifestyle. Ninety-year-old dancer Step Edmonds spoke on the origins of the Cakewalk, "They did a take-off on the high manners of the white folks in the 'big house,' but their masters who gathered around to watch the fun, missed the point."[30] In both examples, we see the signifying monkey at work: the master trickster, altering the production of meaning while appearing to conform to dominant interpretations.

The Whitman Sisters followed in this tradition and produced plantation acts that entertained yet commented on certain perceived social norms, especially the image of Mammy. When Mabel appeared as Mammy with several pickaninnies surrounding her, her behavior was not quite as the minstrel Mammy. This difference is key.

Mammy was an essential member of the fictionalized and idealized plantation life. She was the sentimental counterpart to the old uncle, the docile, obedient happy male slave, the most famous example of which is Uncle Tom. Mammy was the servant matriarch who ran the home, took care of the master's family as well as her own and made sure everybody was happy. She was tough enough to manage the plantation household but tender and devoted to her white charges. Her joy in serving others was romanticized, and she was made into the ideal, faithful domestic servant. Minstrels sang of the joys of coming back to the plantation and seeing Mammy's big bright smile.[31]

Whereas Mammy was warm and loving to her master's family, ensuring that the children were brought up to assume their proper places in white Southern society, she was portrayed as exerting tough love with her own children, whose sole worth was in their economic exchange value.[32] Because Mammy took on the responsibility of overseeing the plantation slaves and making sure all the tasks were completed, she developed an aggressive and independent character. Mammy was headstrong when she needed to be, and, because of her domineering personality, the gender roles were considered reversed in the minstrel family. Mammy was masculinized, given physical characteristics and emotional qualities traditionally attributed to men, while the men (Sambo and old uncle) were given feminized, passive personalities. This construction was used as an argument for the perpetuation of slavery. Pro-slavery activists claimed that one of the many reasons to preserve slavery was that slaves confused gender roles, so they could not be members of society and were therefore better off on the plantation.[33] However, Mammy's aggressive side could alternatively be read as a subversive device. She was able to wield power and get some of what she wanted. Although she was occasionally admonished by her master for being too authoritative, she was usually not crossed, especially not by other slaves. Mammy could sometimes speak her mind freely, which was quite an accomplishment for a slave.[34]

One popular act of the Whitman Sisters presented the familiar scene of a charming Southern cottage at eventide with Mammy peeling potatoes and the children happily singing and dancing. Soon, however, the sisters moved into religious songs that added humanity and depth to their characters and expanded the images beyond stereotypes. In the previous minstrel tradition, a minstrel might sing a song like "Old Folks at Home" by Steven Foster:

> Way down upon de Swanee ribber,
> Far, far away,
> Dere's wha my heart is turning ebber,
> Dere's wha de old folks stay.
> All up and down de whole creation,
> Sadly I roam,
> Still longing for de old plantation,
> And for de old folks at home.
> [. . .]
> All round de little farm I wandered
> When I was young,
> Den many happy days I squandered,
> Many de songs I sung.
> When I was playing wid my brudder
> Happy was I.
> Oh! take me to my kind old mudder,
> Dere let me live and die.[35]

The Whitman Sisters, on the other hand, sang songs from a religious tradition. Although we do not have sheet music from a Whitman Sisters show, we can look at contemporaneous jubilee music for clues to what their songs were like. "Sometimes I Feel Like a Motherless Child" provides a good example:

Sometimes I feel like a motherless child,
Sometimes I feel like a motherless child,
Sometimes I feel like a motherless child,
A long ways from home;
A long ways from home.
True believer, A long ways from home,
A long ways from home.

Sometimes I feel like I'm almos' gone,
Sometimes I feel like I'm almos' gone,
Sometimes I feel like I'm almos' gone;
Way up in de heab'nly lan';
Way up in de heab'nly lan'.
True believer, way up in de heab'nly lan';
Way up in de heab'nly lan',

Sometimes I feel like a motherless child,
Sometimes I feel like a motherless child,
Sometimes I feel like a motherless child,
A long ways from home.[36]

The differences in tone and message in these two examples are apparent. Both songs are about being away from home and longing for a mother figure. However, in the spiritual we see religious overtones in which home represents heaven. We move away from the happy darky longing for the good ol' plantation to the contemplative slave seeking salvation.[37]

The Whitman sisters made similar moves in other aspects of their performances. While mastering stump speeches, breakdowns and coon shouts, all vestiges of minstrelsy, the Whitman sisters also brought class to their shows by singing religious songs, dressing in expensive fashions, and advancing respectable images of African Americans. This juxtaposition resulted in images that conformed to certain expectations on one level, yet did not function as the detrimental stereotypes of white minstrelsy.

Clearly there are many problems involved in a black troupe presenting a minstrel scene with stereotypical characters. So, why did the Whitman

Sisters do it? I believe part of the reason rests in the fact that these scenes were extremely popular with American audiences and therefore made good business sense. By repeating this popular sentimental trope with signal differences, audiences were likely to accept the subtle shifts in representation. Concepts of performance and morality as espoused by feminist theorist Judith L. Stephens are useful here. She interrogates the practice of presenting imagery and ideas in progressive era drama that elevates the "moral value" of femininity.[38] The Whitman Sisters similarly exploited the idea of raising the moral value of their work in terms of both gender and race and were thus able to not only secure a more elevated place for themselves in the social fabric, but also elevate representations of race. This endeavor did not ultimately reinforce the status quo, as Stephens argues occurred with white female imagery in theater at the time. Rather, because dominant ideology placed black women far below white women, creating these images signaled a progression. Although negative images served to create and sustain ideological justification for the perpetuation of race and gender oppression, performers such as the Whitman Sisters who worked an implicit critique of these models into their performances were able to challenge their audiences' expectations in the theater and, perhaps, outside of it as well.

Mabel's adoption of the role of Mammy was quite appropriate in this light. By signifying on this subversive and powerful image and adding respectable religious songs, she was able to both capitalize on and critique this image of black femininity. Mammy may have functioned so as to perpetuate the subjugation of African American women, but by recognizing her for her positive qualities, Mabel proved that this mission backfires. Indeed, contemporary scholars have theorized on Mammy and her complex nature, ultimately reclaiming her. Dickerson reminds us, "The image of the African American woman has been sullied on the world stage. The trick for her now is to reclaim that image through self-definition, using Nommo, the magic power of the word; categorically rejecting the stereotypes which are not 'my shame' (as Harriet Tubman said), they are the shame of the perpetuators."[39] Similarly, in an article for *Ms.* magazine, Alice Walker describes her mother, who was a large (ranging between 250 and 300 pounds) Southern woman who worked as a maid in the homes of white people. Because this description is similar to those of Mammy and Aunt Jemima (an image derived from Mammy), Walker had great difficulty reconciling the image of her mother whom she loved with the image of Mammy whom she was supposed to concurrently accept and reject as a stereotype. She writes: "For generations, in the South it [Mammy] was the only image of a black woman that was acceptable. You could be 'Aunt'

Jemima, sexless and white-loving or you could be unseen."[40] For Walker, the stereotype was reality until she realized that Mammy/her mother was also—and most important—a symbol of nourishment that had existed long before slavery. At this moment of realization, she writes:

> I smiled, for I felt something sweet coming over me. A sureness. A peace. It was, in fact, the belated recognition that I was in the presence of the Goddess. She who nurtures all, and that no matter how disguised, abused, ridiculed She may be, even white supremacists have been unable to throw her away. She is with us still. Furthermore, I realized I loved her.[41]

Some 70 years earlier, the Whitman sisters also saw the possibilities for a positive portrayal of Mammy and used it to their advantage. While signifying on a familiar image, they worked to elevate her status and humanize her. The Whitman sisters also negotiated the complicated issues of race and colorism in their repertory by choosing to not only perform as a black act, but sometimes blacken-up (they would wear burnt cork or greasepaint on their faces) and, in the early years, occasionally perform as a white act—they were fair-complexioned enough to pass.

We know from accounts that the Whitman Sisters did perform in dark makeup.[42] And although there is little documentation about the Whitman Sisters' policy on blacking-up during their shows, there is no evidence to suggest that they blacked-up for certain audiences and not others based on their racial composition. On the contrary, they were champions for integrated audiences and therefore felt that their show was suitably entertaining for white and black audience members alike. The first black minstrels did not black-up, but most later comedians like Williams and Walker found it helpful to contrast the "straight" man with a darker comic. Although no female stars were featured in comedy roles at this time and none adopted the full blackface mask caricature complete with whitened, widened mouths and eyes and white gloves, according to Henry T. Sampson, "It was not uncommon for vaudeville booking agents to encourage very light-complexioned black actresses such as Carita Day, the Whitman Sisters, and Belle Davis to 'darken down.'"[43] Josephine Baker also had to black-up her face in her first appearance in American vaudeville.[44] During the early twentieth century, blacking-up was still prevalent in American entertainment owing to the popularity of ethnic humor (especially white performers doing blackface routines) and the reluctance of critics, spectators, and some performers to let go of certain stock characters and scenarios. Anthony Slide claims that the Whitman Sisters used blackface makeup in part because their fair skin actually hurt their work when they appeared with black male performers, and audience members thought the sisters were white. He argues that audiences were unwilling to accept the notion of blacks and whites sharing a stage, playing opposite each other in romantic roles. He quotes an unnamed 1902 critic who complained that "black men making love to white girls look cheap"[45] and urged all fair-skinned black women to wear blackface makeup on stage to avoid this problem when they appeared on stage opposite black men. It is probably the case that these women blacked-up in both romantic and comedic roles. However, interracial erotic desire was probably seen as more threatening to the established order; playing out the stigma of white and black bodies possibly commingling was dangerous. This was especially the case with black men and white women as the myth of the black male rapist was evoked.

Yet, I argue that based on audience reaction, the play on racial identity and the hint at miscegenation was also intriguing and titillating. By manipulating their racial identity within the repertory, the Whitman sisters challenged their audiences to negotiate racialized expectations.

For example, when audience members saw the white women with blonde hair play opposite dark-skinned men, the taboo/stereotyped fear of black men making love to white women had the potential of being played out in public, and anxiety levels probably rose. However, when the mask was exposed and the blonde women were revealed to be the Whitman sisters, and black, there was probably a collective sigh of relief, a release, laughter. Because the audience hadn't really just witnessed an interracial couple, they could all have a good laugh. I argue, however, that on a deeper level the performers did present an interracial couple. The practice of putting on a persona in a theatrically safe space again allowed the forbidden to be worked out, and an argument for the possibility of interracial romance lay underneath, and myriad reactions probably ensued. If we examine possible responses to an interracial scene, we can see how white women and black men may have identified with the characters. Light-skinned black women may have seen what might happen if they passed for white. Interestingly, dark-skinned black women and white men may have had similar reactions of outrage at a scene that excluded representations of themselves. However, though not represented, white men were not totally excluded from interracial romance. They historically had access to all women; white, white-looking, and dark-complexioned women. Thus, those most excluded from representation in the scenarios were dark-skinned black women.

In another example, the Whitman Sisters performed in black-haired wigs and blackface and then, as a finale, took off the makeup and wigs, let their dyed blonde hair down and came back on stage. This act caught audiences off guard, to say the least. Essie writes:

> The audience was always puzzled and someone was sure to ask, "What are those white women doing up there?" Then they would recognize us as the performers and laugh in amazement.[46]

In this situation, we have black women being mistaken for white women, blacking-up in order to remove the dark mask and appear as black women. Like other light-skinned African Americans, in order to be read as "black," the Whitman sisters had to put on the black mask. Of course, if there were black men on stage when the sisters reappeared as blonde women, the audience's confusion would have escalated due to discomfort about interracial relations.

Applying a black feminist semiotic reading to this puzzled and amazed laughter, I argue that by blacking-up and freely switching between white, light-, and dark-skinned personas, the sisters gave their audiences access to a range of responses through which they could safely and humorously work out anxieties about race and gender. The laughter at the realization was possibly a relief of tension and a return to certainty. Without delving too far into Lacanian psychoanalysis, we can see that audience members clearly experienced a degree of identification with, or at least formed a relationship to the performers. This established relationship was then destabilized when the Whitman sisters altered their appearances and played on gender or race signification. As the Whitman sisters played on expectations of the black female body, they disrupted the gazes of each of their spectators to varying degrees. The answer to the question, "Who are those white women?" was "Black women."

It is quite possible, however, that all audience members did not experience relief of tension in their laughter. For some it may have been a nervous laughter as these spectators wrestled with this disruption in the identification of race. Indeed, others may not have laughed at all. It is possible that white men, for instance, were not returned to a position of certainty. If they experienced pleasure at looking at the Whitman sisters as blonde women and were then upset at seeing black men play opposite these white women, they may have also been angered at being tricked when the mask was revealed. They may have come to the conclusion that they were actually attracted to black women, a feeling with which they might not have been entirely comfortable. The sisters ran the risk of appearing deceitful, but by using the good-natured humor of the final revelation as a safety valve, and by maintaining the company's good name, they were able to reassure their audiences.

While allowing for multiple spectatorships in which different audience members read different meanings into the act of passing, we see that the Whitman sisters nonetheless succeeded in undermining the notion of a fixed racial identity and forced their audiences to reckon with these constructions.

With their effective passing, the Whitman Sisters evoked the practice of many people with "one drop" of black blood who, usually for reasons of social or economic opportunity, lived as white Americans well past emancipation. The practice of passing challenges several assumptions about identity, especially, as Elaine Ginsberg argues, that some identity categories are inherent and unalterable essences. "[P]resumably one cannot pass for something one *is not* unless there is some other, pre-passing, identity that one *is*."[47] Passing also challenges the idea that identity can be read on the body. For example, the actress Abbie Mitchell, who played the lead in *Clorindy* in 1898, was given a choice in life whether to live as an African American or pass. "After her mother's death, Mitchell was offered the option of living with her father's family where she could pass for white. Instead she chose to stay with Mama Alice, the Black woman who had been raising her, and live as a Black."[48] Nella Larsen, a novelist and contemporary of the Whitman sisters, writes about the difference between permanent and occasional passing through the interactions of the characters in her novel *Passing*. Clare chooses to pass completely, not even telling her white husband. Irene passes intermittently at restaurants and some other public spaces in order to get better service but lives in Harlem, devoted to the black bourgeoisie. Irene states:

> It's funny about "passing." We disapprove of it and at the same time condone it. It excites our contempt and yet we rather admire it. We shy away from it with an odd kind of revulsion, but we protect it.[49]

We can also get some clues about the politics of passing from Leonard Reed, a dancer who performed with the Whitman Sisters as a pick with his partner Willie Bryant for a few months in 1926. In *Tap! The Greatest Tap Dance Stars and Their Stories 1900-1955*, he tells stories of almost being "found out" on the white circuits and relates tales of minor blackmail by one of his black valets who threatened to disclose his secret unless permitted to perform. He also tells the story of how he was finally found out. During a two-week layoff from playing white houses, he and Bryant went into black vaudeville houses to keep working and somebody told the white establishments who they were. He goes on to summarize his experiences:

> I don't know whether it was a mistake. I don't regret it. I never thought about whether it was strange going back and forth. I think about it now! I think about the danger, and all the things we did. But after that I never did work white again.[50]

Reed also states that one of the most dangerous aspects of being caught passing was the threat of being caught around white women. The fear of miscegenation outweighed talent and economics. Also, Reed vacillates about whether passing was a mistake. Certainly, he and Bryant reaped many financial rewards for totally passing, but when they tried to be both black and white, their plans backfired.

The Whitman sisters also performed as a white act in their early days.[51] In fact, the Whitman sisters got an early break when talent agents heard them singing and thought they were white.[52] There is no documentation as to the extent to which managers and audiences in the Whitman sisters' early years knew the "truth." At what point they decided to play black houses and fight for desegregation is also unclear; perhaps it was when they began taking on performers who were darker than they. Later, however, the Whitman sisters were able to use their color to their advantage and do something Reed and Bryant were unable to do—that is, to go back and forth between black and white identities, while remaining popular with both white and black audiences. Granted, as women they did not pose the same perceived threat to white women as Reed and Bryant, but their act of passing threatened the hegemony nonetheless.

Stories of passing, for theatrical personalities and others, are numerous and cut to the heart of identity politics in the United States. As Ginsberg writes, "Had emancipation brought full social and legal equality the story of race passing might have ended in the 1860s."[53] But passing, colorism, and identity were complicated negotiations in theater and life. The Whitman Sisters signified on this tradition by passing on stage in order to entertain as well as make their audiences conscious of the ease with which they could step in and out of racial identity. By, in essence, reversing the gaze and taking control of their own representation, the Whitman Sisters adopted what hooks calls an "oppositional gaze"[54] and thereby resisted categorization. Here, the performers took control over their image and forced their audiences to reckon with the implications. Audiences could work out confusion,

Figure 6. Alberta, Alice, Mabel, and Essie.
Reproduced by kind permission of Ernestine Lucas.

nod in complicit understanding at a situation perhaps they or people they knew were in, and wrestle with the intimation that the main criterion for racial judgments and prejudgments, skin color, is nebulous.

In Figure 6 we see the four sisters well dressed and sophisticated, with their hair (though not blonde here) arranged in pompadours. Their race is indeterminable based on a snap judgement, but their style is clear. By participating in the height of fashion, they used style in order to indicate the higher social possibilities available to black women and to solidify their status.

It is also possible that at least Mabel passed in public in order to secure better service and accommodations for the troupe and to avoid problems with certain towns. Henry T. Sampson discusses the practice of using white or fair-complexioned African American advance agents in *The Ghost Walks: A Chronological History of Blacks in Show Business, 1865-1910*:

> Many black shows carried a white manager or business representative who would make all the necessary arrangements with the local theatre manager and the city officials before the arrival of the company. In

some cases light-skinned managers would pass for white to perform the same function.[55]

Because the sisters were light-skinned, they did not have to rely on the usual white male representative.

It is important to mention that along with blacking-up and passing, performing as light-complexioned black women also had its share of complications.[56] In a *Baltimore Afro-American* article, Mabel stated, "You never have a real light colored star on the white stage. When we get too light, as we are (humorously) they won't really welcome you, but still it is a pleasure to know that you are able to qualify as a first class entertainer for that kind of audience."[57] Interestingly, the sisters did not capitalize on the "tragic mulatto" stereotype the way they did the Mammy image. In the minstrel and literary traditions, this sympathetic light-skinned woman was a tragic figure because but for that one drop of black blood, she would have been white. The Whitman sisters may have based this decision on a belief that all black women, no matter what shade, should be considered black women and that the condition of being a black woman was not tragic but something to be celebrated in all of its manifestations.

This is evident in their practices in hiring chorus girls. "The chorus is well drilled and was plainly selected for its youth and beauty as well as for its talent . . ."[58] The chorus lines in the 1920s and 1930s, such as in the shows *The Creole Burlesque Show, Keep Shufflin'* and *The Smart Set*, glorified the light-skinned black woman. This helped to foster and preserve fair-skinned beauty standards as desirable, thus excluding darker women. Even the famed Cotton Club in Harlem was noted for its "high-yellow" chorus line. In 1928, Robert Littel, critic for *The New York Post*, criticized the show *Keep Shufflin'* by comedians Flournoy Miller and Aubrey Lyles for being a copy of a white musical comedy because there was an

> abundance in its ranks of quadroons, octoroons, and even smaller fractions of colored blood. The girls could, most of them, pass as white anywhere. We noted Jewish types, Italian types, and one head of genuine red hair. When they all danced together, the twinkle of their legs was barely a shade darker than the legs of any Broadway chorus.[59]

As Jo Tanner points out, it is ironic that by the 1930s, when the stage image changed from glorified colored girl back to the primacy of "Mammy," these same women had to then blacken-up in order to get roles and conform to certain expectations.[60] Thus, their skin color worked for or against them in different eras.

The Whitman Sisters, in contrast to these other shows, refused to contribute to the proliferation of the light-skinned beauty standard. Even though the sisters themselves were fair, they made it a point to include black women of all different shades in their chorus lines. Jeni LeGon, who got her start on the Whitman Sisters chorus line and then went on to become a great solo tap dancer, stated:

> The Whitman Sisters had fixed the line so we had all the colors that our race is known for. All the pretty shading—from the darkest darkest, to the palest of pale. Each one was a distinct looking kid. It was a rainbow of beautiful girls.[61]

The Whitman sisters were way ahead of their time here by signifying on the ideal images of black femininity and going beyond the cookie cutter standard to promoting individuality in their lines by having multiple skin colors represented. The sisters may have shared some of the colorism that existed in the black community, however. Deborah Kirtman talked about her grandmother Mattie Dorsey (or Mattie Whitman), who was a dancer and "adopted" daughter of the Whitman sisters: "Somewhere in around 1917, she fell out with them, and she felt some of it was related to her dark color, and her forceful personality. However, when my dad was born in 1925, she was back in favor—and my dad's birth is announced in the *Chicago Defender*, February 14, 1925, as 'Burt Dorsey Whitman Scott."[62]

Alice Whitman and the other women in the line capitalized on the power of the erotic in performance with revealing costumes, high kicks, and suggestive hip swinging while they performed Snakehips and Ballin' the Jack. In Figure 7 Alice reveals her leg, and with one hand on her hips and the other touching her shoulder provocatively gazes at the camera. As Audre Lorde noted, the erotic is a source of power for women that is affirming and politically useful even though, for the most part, women have been raised to deny, suspect, and fear this power.[63] These dancing girls, however, learned how to capitalize on the erotic without being labeled loose and without resorting to the contemporaneous burlesque show, which was fast becoming stigmatized for being lewd and morally corrupt. Part of this tactic was the fact that though they swung their hips, which may have been erotic, they did not thrust their pelvises, which would have been considered lascivious.

Part of the Whitman Sisters' strategy for promoting the chorus line included billing the chorus girls more on the strength of their dancing skills

Figure 7. Alice Whitman.
Reproduced by kind permission of Ernestine Lucas.

than for their appearance. They were touted solely as serious dancers and not singer/dancers or comedian/dancers as in previous traditions. By having chorus girls of different shades, the Whitmans helped undermine a stereotype of what was considered beautiful, again focusing audience attention more on the performers' ability rather than physical appearance. Any erotic act was also mitigated by the fact that the dancers were part of a troupe noted for its high moral quality. In fact, the Whitman Sisters may have framed the chorus girl dances with religious singing to soften the impact of the sexual and keep the overall appearance of the show respectable.

Whereas Mulvey sees the erotic as a tool of power used exclusively by the male to objectify the female, Lorde's concept of the erotic, and the Whitman Sisters chorus girls as examples, show that power can rest with the female performer. We see that the erotic in the Whitman Sisters shows, while providing ocular pleasure for audience members, posits control of the gaze, at least partially, in the possession of the female performer. We can recognize that the power rested even more with the female in the case of the Whitman Sisters when we consider the fact that the administrative forces promoting the chorus girls were also female.

Alice in particular was considered quite attractive. In opposition to her baby doll image, Alice also portrayed herself as a sex symbol. Willie Bryant and Leonard Reed both were in love with her, and there were probably others as well. Leonard Reed claims that Alice was "gorgeous" and had "insurance on her legs."[64] As with the issue of race, Alice's performances suggest fluidity. She was able to move between the polar opposites of the innocent and the sex goddess.

The Whitman Sisters also negotiated gender issues in a number of their specialty acts. Essie was featured as a comedian and specialized in a drunk act, traditionally a male line of business. "Essie Whitman, who stands out as a character worker, pleased immensely with her portrayal of a bibulous individual who had taken 'one too many' . . . "[66] She also amazed audiences with her low contralto and her masculine singing.

Alice, "The Queen of Taps," was also in a male line of business and was often the only female tap dancer performing with the picks. Discussing the fact that tap was a predominantly male line of business at the time, LeGon states:

> There weren't too many girl tap acts around . . . You had to tap to be in the chorus line and there were excellent girl tap dancers all over the place. I just don't know why there weren't many soloists. Most of them danced in the chorus or did soubrette out in front of the chorus. But not too many of them went in for doing solo.[67]

By being one of the only black female tap stars, Alice was sending a message about the role of black women in show business. Female performers who became soloists tended to be singers and did not venture into tap dancing. This was due in part to the fact that a female soloist's career as a singer was more secure than as a tap dancer and she did not have to risk her reputation as much. Alice used her cute and vivacious image to break into this line of business. She may have been able to move in more daring ways than her older sisters who maintained the moral backbone of the company. As I stated earlier, LeGon described Alice as a hoofer, meaning not only did she do ladylike dainty tapping as chorus girl tappers did, she also let her weight drop and did the same kind of high-energy, fast-paced, acrobatic tapping that Willie Robinson and the other picks were doing. Alice's skill and willingness to do this kind of specialty act is further evidence of the Whitman sisters' resistance of hegemonic gender models. LeGon states: "There were many women that could 'do it.' Alice Whitman was the best. She was a better dancer than I'd ever be."[68] Leonard Reed claims that Alice, like Bill Robinson, had very clear taps—there was no scraping or shuffling—just a sharp distinct sound.[69]

Alberta practiced gender passing by cross-dressing and adopted the stage name Bert. She became known as the best male impersonator of her time, showing up other male impersonators such as Vesta Tilly, perhaps the most famous British music hall gender bender. Essie tells of a day when Vesta Tilly was supposed to follow Bert on a bill. "[B]ut when she saw Sister's act, she ran out of the theater and wouldn't come back. Sister Bert was the best in the business."[70] The *Indianapolis Freeman* confirms Alberta's popularity:

> The second week of the Whitmans' Repertory Company was better and faster than the first, the principal feature being Alberta Whitman's male impersonation, which was a thriller for this audience. She made some handsome gentleman out doing the original strutter.[71]

Alberta often danced duets with Alice as a boy/girl team, looking much like George and Ada Walker or Johnson and Dean, both famous African American dance duos. In Figure 8 we can see that Alice's image of ravishing femininity is ideally complemented by Bert's dapper man-about-town. Figure 9 is a bill for a pick act that Alberta formed. She was accompanied by three children and in the course of 15 to 18 minutes she changed her male attire 3 times and appeared as 3 different characters. The note penciled in at the bottom says: "We are doing fine." Describing her solo act, Alberta said: "I did flash dancing, throwing my legs every way there was, and I never saw anybody do a strut until after I had already started it."[72] Whereas Alice

Figure 8. "Bert" and Alice.
Reproduced by kind permission of Ernestine Lucas.

was able to do male dancing because she was cute, Alberta could do male dancing because she was dressed as a man. By manipulating dress, voice, walk, name, and mannerisms, Bert was able to alter the signs of identity, and thus alter their signification and significance. This image contrasts with the

BERT WHITMAN
AND HER
"THREE SUNBEAMS"

Real Entertainers   :   Male Impersonation a Specialty

3 Changes of Costumes   :   Time of Act 15 to 18 Minutes

Figure 9. Bert Whitman and Her Three Sunbeams.
Reproduced by kind permission of Ernestine Lucas.

breeches roles in music hall and the nineteenth-century travesty dancer, for whom cross-dressing was, in part, an excuse to get women into short pants to show off their legs and reinforce dominant sexual norms.[73] Because the actual gender of the performer was never in question, when these performers took romantic initiatives or comic liberties, they maintained their femininity and sex appeal. As Senelick states, "When the subservient sex wears the pants, such behavior is condoned only in anodyne modes which contradict the disguise by emphasizing female allure.[74] Male impersonators like Alberta, however, made genuine efforts at illusion by attempting to reproduce authentic male style, fashion, and stance.[75]

An important area of study in contemporary feminist and queer theory has focused on the political meaning of cross-dressing and drag.[76] It is important not to dismiss Alberta's type of drag performance as apolitical simply because it was well received by audiences and critics. True, audiences were not as surprised or threatened by this type of transgression as they were with the sisters' passing for white. It is also the case that Alberta's cross-dressing did not threaten the company's good reputation. As I will show, audiences' responses can be attributed to several factors, and we can, nonetheless, make claims about the disruptive social function of Alberta's cross-dressing.

The overt impact of the act was probably tempered by the religious singing during other parts of the show. Black audiences may also have been able to invoke a model of trickstering as described above and accept that the signs of identity had their meaning altered in the male impersonation. Aware of the fictions of representation in terms of race and cognizant of appearance as an unreliable index of identity, black audiences may have been able to make a similar association with cross-dressing. As a trickster, Alberta was able to take clothes and gesture as signs of gender and confound their messages.

Unlike Mabel passing for white offstage, there is no evidence to suggest that Alberta walked the streets of town dressed as a man. She could only do so on stage. Thus, the theater becomes the only safe space for the performer to step in and out of gender identities as Alberta did.[77] Although not on every vaudeville bill, cross-dressing was still a standard line of business and not an exception (as was race-passing) in early-twentieth-century performance. Vaudeville also offered something for everyone, and a male impersonator act was one of many. Although much more work needs to be done theorizing the history of gender performance, it is important to recognize how drag is political and critical and not just benign style and entertainment. Although most of the work done on gender performance focuses on modern acts and must be placed in this context, and very little work includes cross-dressing on black stages, there are, nonetheless, some general claims we can make about a performance like Alberta's.

During the nineteenth century, glamour drag was more popular than male impersonation but looking at the trends of male impersonation by white women can be helpful in our analysis of Alberta's performance.[78] According to Senelick, male impersonators made these roles accessible to a larger public but not innocuous, as the Atlanta ordinance of 1870 prohibiting performers from wearing the garb of the opposite sex on stage attests. Senelick goes on to claim:

> Homosexual men and women as well as heterosexual transvestites could experiment with gender shuffling in a context that won them approbation and indulgence; the audience could savor sexually provocative behavior because it had ostensibly been neutralized by the transvestitism.[79]

Although Victorian idealism suppressed most of these practices in the name of gentility, it is dangerous to assume that transgressions of sexual norms ceased to exist. As Butler discusses, drag subverts gender norms as well as serves "both the denaturalization and re-idealization of hyperbolic heterosexual gender norms."[80] The drag role requires the performer to quote the accepted conventions of gender behavior and hold these conventions up for critique, making discourse possible. Dolan states, "When the assumed gender role does not coincide with the performer's biological sex, the fictions of gender are highlighted."[81] At the very least, performers such as Bert were able to use the ambivalence of the signs of gender to question the limits of sexual differentiation even while they entertained. Their audiences not only enjoyed the performance but also accepted the broader spectrum of gender identities that cross-dressing implied.

A CLASS ACT ALL THE WAY

AT THE METROPOLITAN

The Whitman Sisters held forth at the Metropolitan Church, on M street northwest, last Monday night. As *The Bee* predicted, they received the greatest ovation at this church of any church in which they have appeared. The Metropolitan Church is the largest in he [*sic*] city; its seating capacity is twenty-five hundred.

The address of Miss Mabel Whitman, the manager, was terse, eloquent, and pathetic. She related incidents of her childhood, and the admonition her father gave the girls before his death, and how they have struggled to maintain their honor and reputation.

The vast audience that cheered this address was an evidence of the esteem and appreciation in which this community holds these young ladies.

They are meeting with success wherever they appear, and those who have not heard them should not fail to do so at the first opportunity.[82]

Mabel's reputation as company manager and the reputation of the entire company rested on audiences' and critics' perception of them as a group of high-class performers. In the above review it is important to note not only that the Whitman sisters played to churches, thereby preserving their moral reputation, but also that Mabel's speech gives us clues into the political negotiation of class at the intersections of race, gender, and performance. In her address to the audience, Mabel made a point to mention the sisters' education and moral upbringing, thereby marking herself, and by extension the company, as part of the growing black cultural elite at the beginning of the twentieth century. Indeed, in the many similar orations and accounts of the family's history that Mabel gave to reporters and audience members, she described in detail the sisters' proper upbringing and education, including musical training and Bible lessons. Reverend Whitman's position as a minister, poet, and strict parent helped secure the sisters' respectable image. By insisting on running their company as a "family," the sisters assured the company's image as high-class quality entertainment by performers of moral rectitude. The sisters were able to maintain this image for decades. Nearly 25 years after the above review, in 1931, Bennie Butler, critic for the *Inter-State Tattler*, wrote:

Mae Whitman, who has successfully guided the Whitman Sisters' musical comedy productions for many, many years, has brought to New York and Harlem in particular, another novel singing, comedy dancing vehicle that lives up to the Whitman trade mark that stands for *high class* entertainment.[83]

The importance of attaining and maintaining high-class entertainment status cannot be understated. Not only did high-class troupes command the respect of audiences and critics, they also commanded higher salaries and more prestige in the entertainment industry. A deeper examination of the particulars of early-twentieth-century social structure is crucial to understanding the class status the Whitman Sisters held in the theater community and larger society.

Class as a social construct is perhaps easier to theorize than race and gender constructions, especially with our late-twentieth-century theories of economics, status, social mobility, and privilege that are tied less to biology than to the work ethic. However, at the beginning of the twentieth century, class was more closely related to biology and the family one was born or married into. For example, a woman's class status was tied to that of her father first and then her husband. African Americans in the United States could not look to the same promise of freedom to improve one's lot in life as whites. Almost no amount of Horatio Algerian bootstrapping could break the economic and social barriers that they faced at every turn. White women could marry up into a higher class or through the death of her husband fall in class standing, but this status was not attained through work at a profession. And the predicament of African American women was exponentially complicated as black women struggled with the compounded politics of race, class, and gender.[84] However, there were some steps that a black woman of this era could take to fashion her image with the goal of attaining the privileges attached to class status. This section examines those steps in general and the particular strategies used by the Whitmans to create and maintain their reputation. They were masters at controlling their public image and rarely were criticized in the press.

Understanding that class, like race and gender, can be read on the body, I argue that Foucaultian notions of disciplining the body can be used here to understand Victorian ideologies of comportment and conformity. Early-twentieth-century racist representations of black women portrayed them as dirty, wanton, and keepers of disorderly households.[85] Due in part to ideologies that held that women were the agents of morality and operated only within the private sphere, black women were held responsible for the rise and fall of the black family and by extension, the entire race.[86] Combined with the racist stereotypical images, these beliefs led many to the false conclusion that black women were to blame for the debased state of the race. For black women who faced these social stigmas, cleanliness, purity, order, and piety were considered external representations of worth and valuable criteria for social judgment; they could be used to combat the biological "determinants" believed to prescribe status.

At a time when eugenics and Victorian notions of social Darwinism were employed to assign African Americans a below-white if not below-human status, many African Americans (across classes) adopted the signs of outward white bourgeois status, including sexual codes, moral codes, material goods, religion, and etiquette. Respectability became an attack on racism, and many African American women used the strategy of re-creating white bourgeois notions of cultured behavior to directly challenge racist definitions. By claiming respectability, these women also claimed humanity.

These black women adopted the tenets of the white Victorian Cult of True Womanhood as standards by which they proved their respectability and worth.[87] The four cardinal virtues of the cult—piety, purity, submission, and domesticity[88]—were upheld by these black woman, who added the category of respectability. By presenting themselves as respectable, poor black women "asserted the will and agency to define themselves outside the parameters of prevailing racist discourses."[89] By constructing their own class identity, these women, in effect, challenged the quasi-scientific biological arguments that purported, through the use of eugenics, genetics, heredity, and phrenology, to claim a secular predestination or biological determinism. These women rejected the beliefs that kept them down by disciplining and claiming control over their bodies.

Respectability became a tool through which African Americans could create an interracial and intraracial class structure as it served to distinguish one class of African Americans from another, as well as to call attention to class similarities between the races. Describing reputable church women, Evelyn Brooks Higginbotham explains:

> While adherence to respectability enabled black women to counter racist images and structures, their discursive contestation was not directed solely at white Americans; the black Baptist women condemned what they perceived to be negative practices and attitudes among their own people. Their assimilationist leanings led to their insistence upon blacks' conformity to the dominant society's norms of manners and morals. Thus the discourse of respectability disclosed class and status differentiation.[90]

In other words, the means by which respectable African Americans asserted their higher-class standings often consisted of defining themselves against the antithesis of respectable ideals, evidenced by, they asserted, the lower classes of their own race. As Higginbotham also observes:

> The repeated references to negative black Others became central to, indeed constitutive of, the social identity of the respectable black American.... If respectability signified dialogue with oneself and with others, it also signified class and status differentiation between those who exhibited its definitional criteria and those who did not.[91]

A challenge for female performers trying to maintain their respectable reputations was the fact that their career choices took them away from the female domain, the home. Female reformers also ventured outside of the home; however, they considered themselves an exception to idealized domesticity. These moral reformers contended that they could weed out corruption and improve society if allowed to extend their housekeeping and sanctifying duties into the public sphere.[92] Similarly, to combat the damaging effects of a public image, female performers such as the Whitman sisters took extra care to create homelike atmospheres by cultivating a family company with themselves as motherly figures, thereby constructing respectable images.

The Whitman sisters' attention to their religious upbringing and their father's status came at a time when black women, through the church, were taking great steps in the battle against racism and for the promotion of racial pride. Higginbotham argues that during the years of escalated racism that followed Reconstruction, women played a major part in expanding the black church and making it the most powerful institution of racial self-help in African American communities. In 1900, black women were able to organize and create the Woman's Convention within the National Baptist Convention. "During these years, the church served as the most effective vehicle by which men and women alike, pushed down by racism and poverty, regrouped and rallied against emotional and physical defeat."[93] Drawing upon the Bible, these women fought for women's rights in the church as well as in the larger society.

It is important to note that African American club women in organizations like the National Association of Colored Women (NACW) as well as church women like those in the Women's Convention of the black Baptist church were extremely dedicated to the politics of respectability. Whereas club women found the need to organize mainly due to white racism, church women were often motivated by the sexism of black men within church organizations. The two groups also differed in attitude toward class stratification. The "lift as we climb" motto of the NACW was criticized by church women as being contemptuous of the poor. The black women's club movement operated with the ideology that black women played a vital role as the foundation for retraining the race and starting the move toward upward progress.

Considering themselves to be part of a "talented tenth," black church women and club women reproduced the values of white middle-class, Protestant America, and operated along class lines, especially with their assimilation of the dominant culture's sexual mores and rules for ladylike behavior. I argue that, even considering the differences stated above, both groups of black women projected respectability as a stark contrast to the racist images of black women provided by the hegemonic culture.

By examining black female leadership at the beginning of the twentieth century, we can clearly see the importance of class status. Members of the female elite were usually educated and often held such occupations as teachers, school administrators, journalists, businesswomen and reformers. They were dedicated to serving the black community.

> They felt that "respectable" behavior in public would earn their people a measure of esteem from white America, and hence they strove to win the black lower class's psychological allegiance to temperance, industriousness, thrift, refined manners, and Victorian sexual morals.[94]

At each town they visited, the Whitman sisters visited women's clubs, officiated at local ceremonies, and associated with the social elite.[95] They were also deeply involved in church activity, and by virtue of their popularity with church audiences it can be concluded that the sisters supported and reinforced the ideologies discussed above. The Whitman sisters used piety as one strategy for combating arguments of biological determinism. For example, in press releases describing the company, it was often noted that Little Pops, Alice's son and budding child star, always crossed himself before he did his act (a habit he preserved throughout his career, incidentally). This observation was meant to serve as testament to the good job the Whitman Sisters did at raising him in a respectable manner. They would have had to work particularly hard to cultivate a religious image for themselves, especially if their preacher father disapproved of their work. Going to church on Sundays was an important way for company members to stay in Mabel's good graces. Donations by the Whitmans were responsible for at least 12 churches being able to pay off their mortgages. For two weeks in 1927, they held a benefit performance for the Grant Memorial A.M.E. Church in Chicago.[96] Clarence Muse offers a somewhat derisive example of the ways in which the Whitmans worked with the church:

> And they still keep up all the old church practices, such as going around and meeting the leaders of each community they play, singing spirituals in church, and putting large sums of money in the collection baskets. Picture the scene for yourself. . . . The church is packed with prospective theatregoers. The old minister is shouting in a sonorous voice, "Little chillun, git on board, dere's room for many mo". The congregation chimes in on the song with all the fervor of an old-time revival. Over the singing of his disciples, the voice of the minister is heard exhorting, "Come on, chillun, young an' old, an' rop yo' nickels, dimes, quarters an' dollar bills in de basket to help put over this rally, so we can burn de mortgage on Easter Sunday mornin'!"
>
> At this advantageous point, Sister Whitman approached the little table in front of the pulpit and ostentatiously places five brand new dollar bills on the table. The preacher noting this, yells out, "Sister Whitman just placed five brand new dollar bills on the table to help us in our rally. God bless you, Sister. Come on, chillun, sing! 'Get on board, Get on board!'" It always knocked the church people over, no matter what they had previously thought of the girls for deserting their father's work.[97]

Though less direct evidence is available, it is also probably the case that the sisters espoused the philosophies of the secular social elite and through their promotion of themselves as part of the upper crust of African American society assisted in the uplift of others by serving as models. This is certainly true if we examine the practice of securing picks. Quite a few children were recruited without parental permission, Mabel tells us, because they were orphans. The sisters "adopted" these talented children, and by thus giving them a good "home" and a decent upbringing, did their part in charity work and uplifting the race.[98] One of the popular stories printed in the papers read:

> In the city of Washington, there was once a little girl whose name was Annie Price, and little Annie—just a kid—weighed only 90 pounds. Everybody had decided that she had about thirty days to live. Well along comes Mabel, and she, with her unerring instinct, saw that the

sickly little weakling had talent and possibilities. As a result, she took the little girl up with her, and gave her a start on a show, meanwhile providing for her medical care and attention such as she ought to have.

The little girl stuck, and today—well just see her in the show with the Four Whitman Sisters and you will see for yourself just what the result was. The little girl has delivered the goods and made a success, and has been accepted everywhere as a favorite, although someone said a long time ago that she was too ugly to live.

That is only one story that can be connected with the Whitmans; there are many others, but space will not permit relating them.[99]

Clarence Muse's commentary offers another opinion of this practice:

They always carried a bunch of clever kids with the show. These, they explained to their audiences, were friendless and homeless orphans. They'd picked them up in their travels and were trying to provide for them after God's commandment. . . . The orphan gag and their so-called charitable efforts to care for them was [*sic*] a tremendous sympathy-getter and helped their business wonderfully.[100]

By raising all of the children and promoting a family atmosphere, the sisters attempted to instill values and morality like those they said their father had given them and prove to the world that the Whitman Sisters deserved a place among the upper echelons of society. Buster Brown remarks on the Whitman Sister's reputation: "I had this idea that show business—and the *Whitman Sisters* was a family show. . . ."[101] The sisters were stern, however, and some of their protégés thought they were too vexatious.

The politics of uplift deserves a closer look in order to understand the complexities of this type of activism and the ideologies behind it.[102] Upper-class African Americans used the rhetoric of racial uplift to battle racist biological determinism with an evolutionary argument for high-status cultural assimilation. This ideology began before emancipation, as black women in the North formed mutual aid societies for poor Southern African Americans and emphasized education to combat racism. During the nineteenth century and into the twentieth, these women expanded their efforts to include employment, suffrage, the defense of black female morality, and the condemnation of lynching.[103] However, as Kevin Gaines notes, "Uplift ideology's argument for black humanity was not an argument for equality."[104] Elite African Americans often made poor African Americans out to be inferior and closer to the minstrel stereotypes in order to prove their worth and participate in the Victorian projects of bettering those below through reform, settlement houses, charity work, and temperance. Combating stereotypes for themselves, these elites used racial hierarchy in terms of social Darwinism to their advantage.[105] There is no evidence to suggest that the Whitman sisters overtly participated in the perpetuation of oppression for lower-class African Americans. However, they certainly distinguished themselves from the lower classes even as they attempted to uplift them.

Du Bois' contemporaneous theories of double consciousness[106] help us understand that these educated blacks often viewed themselves (and other blacks) through the judgmental gaze of whites, even while struggling to break free of falsified white images of blackness into self-consciousness. This, Du Bois argued, is the inner struggle of black middle-class ideology. The contradictions of the class-based project are apparent. Through racial uplift ideology, African American intelligentsia sought to improve the lot of those they considered beneath them even as these upper classes reinforced the perception of the black masses' lower status, all the while seeking the cooperation of white political and business elites in order to create a view of themselves that would meet with the approval of the hegemonic structure.

Gaines argues:

> On the one hand, a broader vision of uplift signifying collective social aspiration, advancement, and struggle had been the legacy of the emancipation era. On the other hand, black elites made uplift the basis for a racialized elite identity claiming Negro improvement through class stratification as race progress, which entailed an attenuated conception of bourgeois qualifications for rights and citizenship.[107]

We can see how the Whitman sisters reinforced and how they challenged the dominant black elite ideology by examining two of the major tenets governing upper-class black female behavior, "true womanhood" and the choice between domesticity and education.

Anna Julia Cooper and many other elite black women of that era argued for the morality of "true womanhood" by advocating a familial, paternalistic structure whereby the man adopts the role of protector and the woman epitomizes the sexual ideologies of chastity, demureness, and even fragility.[108] The Whitman sisters, while presenting themselves as respectable and moral, rejected the notion that they could operate only under the auspices of a man, and were anything but fragile. Their sexuality never became an issue, and their chastity was never questioned in reviews or other public accounts, even if there were any indiscretions going on in their private lives. Though each of them was married at one point or another, the men in the sisters' lives (with the exception of their father) did not take over control of the company or their public image. In fact, at a time when women were often defined by who their husbands were, the Whitman sisters' husbands are barely mentioned in the historical documentation.[109]

The ideology around the image of the true woman necessitated an exclusively private domesticated domain. Many women (black and white) debated the relative benefits of education and public life versus the domestic realm. African American women were by no means monolithic in their responses. Tension increased as the fact that many black women had to work challenged the value of domesticity. The women of the "talented tenth" of black society responsible for the uplift of the race also found many tensions between notions of domesticity, including a woman's place in the home, where she had the most influence, and the values of education and public life. While some of these upper-class women stayed at home with their children, others like Mary Church Terrell, Ida B. Wells, and Mary McCleod Bethune opted first and foremost for education, often marrying later and having fewer children in order to lead active public lives speaking out for racial improvements.[110]

In the attempt to reconcile the two sides, some black women activists such as Cooper fought for the education of black women as well as promoted the place of black men as the protector of black women.[111] Their argument held that some women are intended for family life, others for public work. Cooper stated, "We can't all be professional people. We must have a backbone to the race."[112] Many black women struggled with the choice between activism and domestic roles.[113] Schools developed for African American women's training in domestic work, instructing students how to keep the home in proper order and to work as domestics in the homes of whites. The irony of training for domestic work is obvious; many of these women would have to leave their own homes, thus deserting part of the ideal of womanhood, in order to work in white people's homes.[114]

The Whitman sisters were able to prove that they were intended for both family life and public work. The family company was the ideal vehicle for them. While refusing to sacrifice their academic credentials and intellect and despite the fact that only Alice had a biological child, the sisters, as surrogate mothers for young entertainers, were able to furnish a home life while becoming public successes, thus securing for themselves positions in perhaps the best of both worlds. As we see again in the 1908 *Washington Bee* article, the Whitman sisters were very adept at this negotiation between the public and the private:

> The Whitman Sisters are making fine runs in Chicago and meeting with great success. This is gratifying and proper; these people are no fakes, but strong, intelligent, Christian people from one of the Negro families in the South, and their plays and renditions have never been surpassed in Chicago. . . . They are good and intelligent people. Encourage them.[115]

It is important to examine the ways in which class ideologies influenced the structures of the theater community as well as the larger society. In many ways, the hierarchical social structure influenced or was mimicked by the performance structure. In other words, the type of theater one liked was a good indication of one's social status.

As Lawrence Levine discusses in *Highbrow/Lowbrow: The Emergence Of Cultural Hierarchy In America*, the desire to promote entertainment as respectable in the late nineteenth and early twentieth centuries resulted when American society created cultural hierarchies, dividing performance into high/low categories, each with its own implications. Cultural leaders deemed themselves the arbiters of taste and the established authorities on theaters, actors, orchestras, musicians, art museums, and audiences. Rules for proper behavior were instituted and enforced. In order to legitimate the industry, "art" was distinguished from "entertainment" and commanded higher admission prices. Even within the lower forms of entertainment, hierarchies arose so that some establishments were considered more wholesome and refined than others. No longer was it acceptable in highbrow venues for audience members to throw fruit, hiss, or even talk during performances—all previously sanctioned behaviors. In vaudeville, white male producers such as Tony Paster, B. F. Keith, Edward F. Albee and F. F. Proctor endeavored to make the vaudeville house a venue for decent family entertainment. The Keith theaters were nicknamed "the Sunday School Circuit," and as Snyder articulates:

> Keith mastered and exploited a rhetoric of cultural refinement and moral elevation to legitimate a new kind of theatre. In a time when legal restraints and regulations still shadowed the stage, the "Sunday School Circuit" reputation could soothe the anxieties of moral reformers and attract family audiences. Self-censorship meant bigger audiences and bigger profits.[116]

Vulgarity and baseness of all sorts were banished and replaced by courteousness and decorum. Class structures for performances were reorganized along cultural lines and adjectives like "high-class" and "low-class" were applied.

This high/low dichotomy developed in the African American community as well. Juke joints, rent parties, and some types of traveling shows qualified as low-class entertainment. The venues for these types of entertainment were usually makeshift, admission prices were cheap, and the performers were often less skilled than in high-class establishments. To reach high-class status, performers had to not only be talented but also had to prove their respectability by exuding sophistication, elegance, and morality.

African American women in show business had even more to overcome than their non-performing counterparts. As Ethel Waters explains, these women had a serious legacy with which to contend as black women in earlier shows and carnivals "were considered not much better than cattle by respectable Negroes."[117] Several performers, including the Whitman sisters, were masters at altering this image and presenting themselves as the pinnacles of class. On the stage, the dance team of Johnson and Dean was considered the first black "class" act. Dressed in evening clothes, portraying themselves as a courtly gentleman and a gracious lady, they were the first black dance team to play on Broadway. Known as the black Venus, Dora Dean was fair-complexioned, had an hourglass figure and wore $1,000 gowns on stage. By presenting the privileged body on stage in expensive clothes and by moving with sophistication, these performers used the politics of respectability to their advantage and created high-status images for themselves. The juxtaposition of dark skin with elegant costumes and mannerisms was one strategy for elevating the images of African Americans.

The Whitman sisters did not perform operas or "serious singing" like Sissieretta Jones, Elizabeth Taylor Greenfield, Anna Madah Hyer, or Mme. Marie Selika; nor did they perform in "legitimate" theater like Henrietta Vinton Davis. Nonetheless, they were considered high-class entertainers and were respected. They maintained this status by not only creating a family atmosphere for the company, touring as a featured act on the Family United circuit and at the Standard (bastions of legitimate vaudeville) but also by enforcing strict rules on their company. The Whitman sisters used a strategy similar to Johnson and Dean when it came to costuming. On stage, their costumes were well tailored and elegant. They also arranged their programs so that they pleased a wide variety of audience members, sang religious songs, toured respected black churches where they were invariably well received and made generous donations. "Every church of any promi-

nence [was] opened to these artists."[118] The significance of churches opening their doors to vaudeville performers cannot be understated. It was a
societal seal of approval which the sisters used extensively in their publicity.

In several ways, the Whitmans' work met the politics of class and
respectability. These negotiations of status and image can help us further
understand the importance of their accomplishments.

For example, in 1914, the Women's Convention and the NAACP joined
forces to protest negative stereotyping of blacks in literature, film, school
textbooks, newspapers, and on the stage.[119] "The exaltation of domestic
virtue, symbolized by home, family, chastity, and respectability, all infused
with an ethic of religious piety, provided the moral criteria for uplift's cultural
aesthetic."[120] The black elites, therefore, rejected jazz and secular dancing as
morally debased. Jubilee songs, spirituals, and nostalgic plantation songs that
portrayed proper Victorian sentimentalism were lauded by elite African Americans, whereas the more vulgar "coon songs" were decried as low and undig-
nified and given no place within the cultural aesthetic.[121] But these "lower"
musical forms were extremely popular with a broader base of spectators and
led to the success of black musical comedies. The Whitmans negotiated a
precarious position trying to maintain their popularity as well as their high-
class status. They were able to mix coon shouts and jubilee sorrow songs,
breakdowns, and Cakewalks. By presenting familiar characters removed from
the damaging negative stereotypes, as discussed in the previous section, the
Whitmans were able to appeal to a wide range of spectators.[122] Keeping a
large repertory of acts on hand may have proven beneficial in planning a
performance as they would have been able to shift the tone of the evening
between respectable and popular depending on venue. No matter who the
target audience was, however, as Lucas says, "Theirs was to be a show of
quality, the very best they could produce."[123] Always high-class in their off-
stage public life, however, they were always well dressed and stayed away from
low-class establishments. They visited churches often even when they were
not performing to make generous contributions and emphasized the family's
respectable history when interviewing with reporters. These noble off-stage
acts operated as a way of conditioning upper-echelon audience responses to
their flirtation with lower-class forms on stage. The sisters' reputability secured
them a place from which they could contest dominant stereotypical images
on stage. By playing to both popular theaters and churches, the Whitman
sisters were able to reinforce black elite ideals as well as capitalize on popular
performance.

Gaines discusses how some black performers such as Bert Williams
used minstrel formulas to gain access to white audiences. Elite blacks, on the

other hand, were trying to counter such stereotypes, while basing their authority on racialized conceptions of bourgeois morality.

> Specifically, elite blacks celebrated the home and patriarchal family as institutions that symbolized the freedom, power, and security they aspired to. Through their frequent tributes to home and family life, African Americans laid claim to the respectability and stability withheld by the state and by minstrelsy's slanders.[124]

The Whitman sisters' overarching strategy for negotiating these class and racial lines and for remaining both popular and elite rested in their masterful ability to remain loyal, in essence, to everyone. Other companies may have had different types of acts, but it is clear from the Whitman Sisters' success that they were among the best at negotiating these lines. The Whitmans managed to create shows that pleased a multitude of possible spectators across society's subsections—white and black, male and female, rich and poor—without betraying loyalty to any particular group. For example, on the same bill one might have heard jubilees, which would have appealed to a high-class crowd, as well as coon shouting and jazz music, which would have been recognized as lower class. The high-class Cakewalk shared the stage with hoofing. Women would have liked listening to the sentimental sorrow songs while men probably enjoyed the dancing girls. In the "befoh da wah" scenes whites may have simply seen another minstrel routine while blacks may have picked up on the more dignified portrayals of African American life. And everybody loved the picks.

　　For a black performer at the turn of the century, maintaining high-class status while performing race was a complex negotiation in terms of allegiance. A vocabulary of "yours" and "ours" had developed in the larger society as African Americans placed their high achievers on pedestals as representatives of their race's potential. As Jack Johnson proved with boxing and Sissieretta Jones proved with opera, African Americans were not only as qualified as whites, but often beat them at their own games. The Whitman sisters managed to become representatives of their race while remaining popular with white audiences. Black audiences did not believe the sisters sold out to white money and fame as they assumed other black artists had done. By playing to white audiences, the sisters increased their popularity and their revenue; indeed, it probably would have been financially impossible to ignore this audience base. Their hearts, however, were with African American communities. The ways in which the Whitman Sisters maintained this balance of appeal and played to these two audiences illustrates W. E. B.

Du Bois' theories on double consciousness, the necessity of understanding and presenting the self as two, one American and one Negro. Because black and white spectators shared the same house, African American performers like the Whitman sisters had to be able to "play to" different audiences members simultaneously.[125] This practice was politically informed as these performers were able to renegotiate the boundaries of race, class, and gender by presenting respectable images that entertained while resisting stereotypes. As David Krasner points out:

> Within the same show at times, black performers would simultaneously accommodate and resist the dominant culture. However, there is no denying that black performers and writers felt the sense of doubleness keenly, and they worked adroitly within the limited spaces available to challenge the tide of racism.[126]

By 1918, the Whitman sisters had successfully toured most of the major white vaudeville theaters and circuits in the United States, including the Orpheum, Kohl & Castle, and Keith & Proctor. In 1925 they briefly played the white Gus Sun Time Circuit and in 1928 they played the Publix Theatre Circuit. However, throughout their careers they were able to maintain loyalty to their black audiences. A *Chicago Defender* reporter writes:

> Both as to ability and personality these young ladies are thoroughly qualified to attach themselves in a line of activity which would take them entirely away from "our people" but, despite the efforts made by many managers to effect this result, we still are proud to say that we have them with us.[127]

Another reporter who recognized the Whitman Sisters' loyalty to African American communities said, "I gathered the impression, too, that the Whitmans work much harder to satisfy their own people than they do for others, and there seems to be no question about it, judging from records."[128]

Mabel also emphasized the group's commitment to the African American communities despite their success with white audiences. In 1931, she claimed:

> I think beyond question that a colored audience is our favorite, for there we get full appreciation . . . give us a colored audience any old day in the week."[129]

We can probably believe Mabel when she claims that the sisters preferred African American audiences. After all, the Whitman sisters did have opportunities to play exclusively white houses, but by choosing to identify themselves with the black community, the Whitman Sisters attained the status of royalty.[130] Their strategies of respectability, uplift, and true womanhood paid off handsomely.

A WOMAN OF GREAT EXECUTIVE ABILITY[131]

Once in every generation comes a person whose magnetism, charm, force and personality make them outstanding in the careers they choose themselves, and such a personage is Mabel Whitman, manager, pro-ducer and co-owner, along with her other sisters of the famous Whit-man troupe.[132]

About the sisters themselves, Mabel, popularly known in the profession as "Sister Mae" (a name she seems to love) is the "big sister" of all the folks in her shows as well as being the general manager and producer. It is she who toils with the younger actors and actresses just breaking in and helps them iron out the rough spots. And believe me, when she finishes with them, a darn good job has been done.[133]

The Whitman sisters' careers lasted more than 40 years. The company started in the wake of the Depression of 1893, survived World War I and the Great Depression of the 1930s, and folded just before the United States entered World War II. The success and longevity of the company was due in large part to the efforts of Mabel Whitman, who stopped performing for many years in order to manage the company. Rather than hiring outside the family, the sisters took on all production responsibilities themselves. Mabel took care of all of the bookings and business; Essie designed and made costumes; and Alberta was financial secretary and composed music for the show. In 1904, Mabel Whitman was said to have been the only black woman managing her own company and booking them at the best Southern venues. Mabel's status as female entrepreneur and independent manager-owner of the Whitman Sisters was an exception to the rule, and she offered a rare opportunity for black performers to work for a black manager in a black show. According to Bill Reed, "no finer actor-manager ever existed than the act's unquestioned leader, Mabel Whitman."[134] Known for her clever busi-ness dealings, at least one *Chicago Defender* reporter nicknamed her "Tiger Show Woman."[135] A reporter for the *Pittsburgh Courier* writes:

> Managers and theatre-owners all over the country have tales to tell of
> how the wily "boss" of the Whitmans pulled a fast one on them—and
> made them like it. Nothing underhanded, but just shrewd business.[136]

"(G)rab every new idea, speed, pep, originality and—pretty girls."[137] This is
what it took to "go over" or succeed in the show business game, and Mabel
Whitman was a master. In this section I analyze her strategies for success
despite the forces operating against her. A rare photograph of Mabel seated
alone (Figure 10) captures Mabel's stature and elegance. Signs of respectability
can be read in her stoic facial expression, her long dress, the tasteful pearls,
and the contained comportment in the solid hardwood chair with its regal
high back and coat of arms. One gets the sense that everything is in its place,
under control, and that she is, as Thorpe, Johns, and the Stearnses have all
called her, a "formidable" woman. Mabel's success in a business dominated by
white men is further evidence of the important contribution of the Whitman
Sisters to theater history and deserves a closer look.

> Miss Whitman is described as the most daring woman in the show
> game, and her exceptionally keen showmanship, fit to stand beside the
> exceptional entertainment material which she is always able to assem-
> ble, has placed her head and shoulders above the ruck.[138]

To put Mabel Whitman's achievements as a manager in proper contexts we must first review the development of the vaudeville business and
circuits. During the Panic of 1893, six white managers—Marc Klaw,
Abraham Erlanger, Al Hayman, Charles Frohman, J. Frederick Zimmerman,
and Samuel Nixon—united and founded the Trust, or Syndicate, which was
a circuit of theaters specializing in variety and musical productions. By 1896,
the Trust controlled more than 500 theaters throughout the United States.
Consolidation allowed these men to regulate bookings, set efficient financial
standards, and effectively dissolve the actor-manager system. However, the
Trust was also known for censorship and unscrupulous management practices. According to Riis, syndicates like the Trust provided work for many
black performers at the turn of the century because economic prejudice
prevented these black performers from ever becoming independent
manager-owners of their own companies.[139] Unable to manage their own
companies, however, these performers were often at the mercy of these
disreputable and usually racist men who had them work in deplorable
conditions and paid them less than their white counterparts. Between the
Trust and the White Rats, an association of white performers who opposed

MISS MABEL WHITMAN
with "The Old Team" Company

Figure 10. Mabel Whitman. Reproduced courtesy of the Billy Rose Theatre Collection,
The New York Public Library for the Performing Arts.
Astor, Lenox, and Tilden Foundations.

the booking of black performers on major white vaudeville circuits,[140] black performers had little control over their careers.

African American managers like P. T. Wright, who organized the Nashville Students, O. M. McAdoo, who took the first black companies to South Africa and Australia, and Harry Eaton, who put out the first vaudeville specialty company, had operated theatrical companies since the 1890s. In the 1910s, when black theater ownership increased, mostly because of segregation and black Southern enterprise, black syndicates for traveling shows were formed. Because black acts were so popular, white syndicates were committed to booking them, and African American theater owners always had competition from white syndicates that had more financial clout and could pay more for the best acts. For example, Sam Lucas, a black minstrel, suggested the idea of *The Creole Show*, but it was Sam T. Jack, a white manager, who ran the show.[141] Even the famous opera singer Sissieretta Jones, who toured with her Troubadours group, and the *Smart Set* touring show were managed by white members of the Trust.[142] Against this grain, Mabel was able to book the Whitman Sisters in some of the best houses, demand top dollar, garner the best acts, fight corruption, and desegregate theaters. Mabel successfully took on the Trust, offering some of the best black performers an alternative model. Mabel ran the Whitman Sisters' operation alone for more than 20 years, and even when the company joined the black circuit in the 1920s Mabel still made decisions regarding the company's bookings and compensation.

To unpack the significance of Mabel's management practices we must interrogate the sociopolitical implications of being a black female vaudeville manager in the early part of the twentieth century. In three important ways, Mabel confronted and resisted the standards constructed by other management models, and these confrontations allowed her to succeed despite many obstacles. Mabel's strategies included hiring the best performers by providing a family environment; desegregating theaters; and publicizing and fighting corruption in show business. Mabel took two seeming handicaps, her race and gender, and turned them to her advantage by becoming the stern and authoritative matriarch of the company. The theater's reputation for being considerably less than respectable and actresses' reputations for being morally suspect often prevented black mothers from allowing their children (especially their daughters) to leave home and join a show.[143] There were countless tales of young hopefuls falling prey to licentious show people, and black parents were understandably wary.

Mabel, however, had a distinct advantage over white theater managers when it came to securing these popular child acts. By adopting the role of matriarch, Mabel Whitman was able to assure black parents that their talented children would be protected with the Whitman Sisters; this was a promise that none of the male managers in competition could offer. She also served as a role model for her charges, especially the girls. In a 1924 interview Mabel stated, "The girls look to me for everything. I am the 'ma' of the crowd."[144] Catherine Basie recounts: "Any mother could tell you that if your daughter was with The Whitman Sisters, she was safe."[145] This allowed the Whitman Sisters to establish some of the best child acts in vaudeville.

Not only did the sisters raise, educate, and instill religious values in the children, they also protected them from harmful temptations. Young performers were not permitted to drink or smoke. The girls had to ride separately with one of the sisters (they could not ride with the boys), and only the married couples could live together. If anybody broke these rules guiding sexual conduct, he or she was immediately sent home.

As a surrogate mother, Mabel commanded respect. Aaron Palmer, one of the Dixie Boys, said: "May Whitman was just like a mother to me."[146] Dancer Joe Jones claimed that when he joined the troupe at seven years old he was scared to death of Essie and Mabel because they had deep voices like men and could spank "really hard" in order to keep the children in line. Leonard Reed left the show after an argument with Mabel in 1929 over artistic differences. According to Reed, he and Willie were inhibited from doing too much for fear of upstaging Pops.

Ultimately, however, children working with the Whitmans were well educated in performance. According to Leonard Reed: "The Whitman Sisters were a real school for young talent. . . . I learned a lot in the Whitman Sister's show."[147] Reed stayed with the sisters for four months and met his partner Willie Bryant with the troupe. Willie was older and taught him a soft shoe and other moves.

Mabel's practice of "adopting" young children and treating them as members of the family was not only an important business strategy, it was also part of a tradition of African American extended family kinship.[148] Elmer and Joanne Martin describe this practice as "absorption and informal adoption"[149] whereby mothers and other mothers share responsibility for raising a child. African American families have a long tradition of communal child care and surrogate mothering. The Whitman sisters functioned as mothers, and the company was structured as an extended family in which all members were protected.[150] Gerda Lerner's explanation of the development of these female-headed extended families is useful in understanding the company's management philosophies. She states:

> Although from the late 19th century to today at least 75 per cent of all black families *were* nuclear families headed by a male, there also developed another black family pattern, that of the extended family.... This family structure, in which all children, regardless of the marital status or economic status of their families, are ensured a modicum of security, represents a useful adaptation for group survival.[151]

Although attaining good child acts was a priority for the Whitman Sisters, the adult acts were also very popular. The company's family atmosphere would have also appealed to adults, especially female performers, interested in being associated with a respectable theatrical institution that would protect their reputations. Working with a reputable company like the Whitman Sisters that provided excellent apprenticeships was a good start to any performer's career, child or adult.

The second way Mabel resisted standard management models was by fighting to desegregate theaters. Ever since African Americans broke into show business, racism in the theater industry had to be negotiated in the practical terms of travel arrangements and accommodations. By the 1870s, the "Jim Crow" laws were chipping away at any civil rights that African Americans had obtained during Reconstruction. These segregation laws applied not only to restaurants, trains, and schools, but also to entertainment venues. African American performers often had problems touring when hotels, restaurants, and trains refused to accommodate them. To avoid complications brought on by this institutionalized racism, Mabel took steps to provide for the company. She made sure that the company members traveled together and made arrangements for accommodations well in advance.

"Nigger Heaven" was created in the balcony of theaters to keep audiences segregated when African Americans were admitted to performances at all. On July 11, 1904, after the sisters had only four years of performing professionally, Mabel Whitman insisted that black patrons be allowed to sit in the dress circle and parquet sections of the Jefferson Theater in Birmingham, Alabama.[152] She got her demands, and for the first time in the history of the town, theater segregation codes were challenged and overturned.[153] It is important to note that this protest took place at a time before large efforts at desegregation were being attempted. Allen Woll claims that occasional protests against these policies were made in 1910. He cites several incidents in which black patrons obtained tickets in the lower levels, usually by sending a white messenger, and then attempted to take their seats, usually unsuccessfully. It was not until 1912, however, that national court action was taken to effect desegregation in theaters. F.

Baldwin, with the help of the NAACP, sued the theater that removed him from his seat; he won but received only $50 in compensation.[154] Large-scale efforts did eventually lead to integration, but Mabel's efforts in 1904 must be recognized as an important early fight for desegregation.

Segregation was not the only racist practice that African American performers faced. There were many shady dealings in show business at the beginning of the twentieth century. Racism ensured that black performers would always have a difficult time obtaining fair treatment. For example, black showmen Cole and Johnson stopped producing big shows in 1910 because, they said, booking agents and producers refused to book black shows in first-class theaters. In September 1913, manager S. H. Dudley faced a similar situation and, pointing to institutionalized racism, said he did not want to book "first-class entertainment in second-class theaters."[155]

Not only was Mabel an excellent manager thanks to her skills at procuring acts, she also insisted on booking the company at the best venues and was not afraid to speak out against racist and corrupt practices in the vaudeville industry. Mabel was a tireless champion for the rights of black patrons and performers. She broke many race and gender barriers in theater management practices by insisting on *at least* the same standards as white performers in terms of accommodations and salary and by taking drastic steps when she perceived unfair treatment because of her or company members' race or gender. It was clear to everybody in the business that Mabel Whitman would not and could not be exploited because she was a black woman. In an interview in the *Baltimore Afro-American*, Mabel discussed in detail the problems she faced working with racist and corrupt theater owners and managers. This rare firsthand account deserves to be quoted at length:

> The trouble with this game is a set of unscrupulous owners and managers who seemingly have syndicated themselves together to stifle the progress along the lines of art and entertainment. They feel that any kind of show is good enough for a colored audience and their only desire is to have a comedian and a few half-naked girls on hand to keep the doors open.
>
> They insult the intelligence and prey on Negro patrons. They sense that the people must have some place to go for amusement; instead of giving them the best talent possible, they palm off the worst as long as they can.
>
> When the crowd gets fed up on that sort of diet, they try to work a good show and try to get it for the same money they pay an amateur company which was made up overnight. This is what a certain owner

told me—and I'll name him when and if necessary—"I have been losing money all year and I have to get out of the red on your engagement here. Therefore I won't pay you what you want. You have a family company. You don't need money because you all work and live together. Come in at my price or stay out."

Well I stayed out. I am staying out and I never in life will pay for a man who tells me I have to foot the losses he has suffered from bum shows.

Let me give you some figures in this particular case. Years ago, when I had a smaller show, he refused to pay me a guarantee of $1400. I went in on a percentage and took away $2700 for my end of the receipts. The last time we played his house my cut for the week was $3750. Then, when he tried to get me this fall, he offered me a guarantee of $1600 instead of the usual percentage and explained himself by saying that I, Mae Whitman, had to make up for the bad weeks other people had given him.

He offered me $1600 for a company of 30 people. He offered me $1600 and it would cost me $490 in railroad fare, exclusive of baggage transportation, to get there. (Excuse me if I am not as calm as usual.)

What encouragement does a producer get out of that sort of stuff? How can you improve and develop your shows and people if there is no more money available for a good show than for a misfit outfit?

This is what an owner did here in Philadelphia. He went to the individual members of a show in his house and asked them what their salary was, offering as an excuse that he was about to produce a show and wanted to use them in it. At the end of the week he paid off the performers himself and paid the producer a musician's salary.

What does "Mabel Whitman" mean to men of that type? Does my name stand for anything with them? For no more than "Mabel Jack Rabbit"?

But there is another picture, a bright and cheerful one. All owners are not in that category. In this game there are men who appreciate your work and your worth. They try to give their patrons leading entertainment and you always work harder for such managers. Believe me, twenty years experience by Mae Whitman means something to them. . . . That's why, in the course of a season, we play from two to eight weeks with Mr. Gibson and other high-class theatrical men.

And now do you know what is the matter with show business?[156]

On another occasion, the management of the Regal Theater in Chicago tried to take advantage of the Whitman Sisters when they discovered the company to be managed by a black woman and decided to pay the company less than what they had agreed upon. According to the Stearnses, Mabel "walked across the street to the Metropolitan Theater, which lacked a stage, had a new stage built, opened with a different show, and ruined the Regal's business for two weeks."[157] Samuel Hay tells another story of the Whitman Sisters teaching a lesson to the racist white owner of a high-class theater. Right before a performance, the sisters heard that the owner would not pay the agreed-upon price because it was equal to what he paid his white acts. Knowing that their acts were better than the white companies', Mabel demanded the agreed-upon amount in advance. The owner offered a compromise, but Mabel told him that they would not play for him for any amount of money and left.[158] This may seem a high price to pay for principles, but Mabel quickly gained respect and a reputation for being a shrewd manager who would not be exploited because of her race or gender. Mabel's management strategies kept the company running for a long time. Unfortunately, the same cannot be said for other African American shows. As early as 1910, many of the most popular black stars were no longer performing in large-scale black shows. Broadway lyricist James Weldon Johnson called the next seven years, the "term of exile"[159] for African Americans on Broadway. These black performances waned until the start of the Harlem Renaissance. As Allen Woll describes:

> Ernest Hogan, Bob Cole and George Walker were dead. Will Marion Cook, James Weldon Johnson and J. Rosamond Johnson had pursued new interests or careers. And the giant of them all, Bert Williams, had moved to the Ziegfield Follies.[160]

Although many black performers moved from the theatrical epicenter of New York to regional black vaudeville, conditions there were not much better. In fact, the situation was so bad in "colored show business" with lack of financial sponsorship, second-class bookings, and racism, that it was often better to join a white circuit (if one could get hired) than to star in a colored show. Again refusing to play white circuits exclusively, Mabel ensured that the Whitman Sisters not only survived these difficult times, but thrived. The Smart Set and Black Patti's Troubadours were the largest remaining black touring companies in 1910 (along with minstrel shows and "Tom" shows). The Whitman Sisters was probably the third- largest show, but had the distinction of being the only company owned and managed by an African American woman. Mabel so successfully managed the company that it outlasted all of the others, playing well into the 1930s.

TOBY, the Depression, and Beyond: The Later Years

High Class Musical Comedies and Road Shows Always in Demand: The Largest Circuit for Colored Companies in America[1]

WHILE THE HARLEM RENAISSANCE was flourishing in major Northern cities, another story of black cultural production was unfolding in other parts of the country. In the early 1920s, the Whitman Sisters joined the black vaudeville traveling circuit TOBA, which alternately stood for Theatre Owners' Booking Association, Tough on Black Actors, and Tough on Black Asses. According to poet Langston Hughes, the circuit was thus nicknamed because it paid very little money, except to headliners such as the Whitman sisters. Those with top billing got work 52 weeks a year at good salaries. Hughes identified some of the most famous headliners as The Whitman Sisters, singer Bessie Smith, Butterbeans and Susie, comedian S. H. Dudley and his mule, and comedian Tom Fletcher.[2] This circuit was also referred to as The Chitlin Circuit and the title I use here, Toby.

Theater historians generally recognize the advent of talkies and the worsening Depression of the 1930s as bringing the end of American vaudeville.[3] An examination of black American vaudeville reveals another scenario, however. These performers made alternate choices in order to adapt, and the Whitman Sisters were perhaps the most successful. By examining the later years of the Whitman Sisters' vaudeville troupe, we can investigate how these choices enabled the company to remain successful well into the late 1930s and leave a legacy for the next generation of performers and spectators.

Traveling companies became more predominant than resident stock companies in black entertainment just after the Civil War. Because of increasing organizational complexities, booking agencies were needed and group agreements were made. Thomas Riis explains, "Circuits of theaters with a single owner emerged and prospered."[4] I have already discussed the white theater circuit in the late nineteenth century; it was not until the early 1910s, however, that a major black vaudeville circuit emerged catering almost exclusively to an African American clientele. In 1912, black vaudeville comedian Sherman H. Dudley moved to Washington D. C., went into semiretirement from performing, and started leasing and buying theaters.[5] He worked with several white and black theater owners in the South and together with producers Martin Klein, E. L. Cummings, Milton Starr, and about 15 investors, was instrumental in forming Toby.[6] By the 1920s, Toby theaters were in most areas of the South, Southwest, and Midwest, with a few in the North. By 1921, Toby was well represented in Galveston, Jacksonville, Cleveland, Kansas City, St. Louis, Nashville, Chattanooga, Memphis, New Orleans, Durham, and Baltimore, among other major cities.

A few Toby shows had semipermanent resident companies. The Grand on Chicago's Southside had a musical stock company, headed for a time by the comedian Billy King, and in Atlanta, S. H. Dudley had a company in which the young comedian Nipsey Russell honed his craft. It is also important to mention that Toby was instrumental in popularizing blues and jazz. Indeed, without Toby, Ma Rainey, Bessie Smith, and other blues greats would have had few theaters in which to perform, gaining reputations that would allow them to go on to make records. Thus, we may never have heard recordings of these remarkable singers without Toby.[7]

The vast majority of performers on Toby were part of touring shows. A company on Toby traveled second-class trains to each city or small Southern town. Costumes and sets were minimal, and the house band provided musical accompaniment. The most popular acts were center-stage singing and lowbrow "blue" comedy routines, although blue material was censored in some towns. Twenty-five cents bought a spectator admission to the show and a raffle ticket for a door prize—often a gold tooth. A press release flyer states, "An occasional ham or turkey would never cause as much 'checking the number on your ticket' as a gold tooth."[8] Clarence Muse describes a typical Toby show as tabloid editions of musical comedies. Three shows were performed nightly, each about 45 minutes, and the company for these revues had approximately 35 people. In addition to the low salaries, small-time performers often had to contend with poor theater and housing conditions, haphazard scheduling, cramped and makeshift dressing areas, poor lighting and staging, cheating managers, and racism. The possibility of severe racist treatment by townspeople and even lynchings kept many performers away from Toby, as they preferred to deal with the less brutal form of Northern racism. Southern "hospitality" especially troubled the many midlevel performers who stayed with Toby, as travel and housing arrangements often could not be made, forcing these performers to stay in train stations where they could easily be attacked by angry mobs.[9] According to Sampson, performers often dressed in plain clothes, appearing as field hands or domestics so as not to draw attention to themselves as performers. One of the most tragic incidents occurred when Louis Wright of the Georgia Minstrels was lynched by a mob after refusing to ignore an insult from a white resident of a small town in southeastern Missouri.[10]

The Whitmans may have also faced some hard times on Toby, though undoubtedly fewer than small-time performers. Leonard Reed tells of being on the road performing with Travis Tucker in the Whitman Sister's show. Because he and Travis couldn't pay their rent, he dropped their bags out of the window to Alberta, while Travis stalled the landlady with promises of payment. Hotels at this time were in the habit of "attaching" trunks. They would take a performer's trunk to the police station who refused to return the trunk until all debts were paid. Travis and Reed would circumvent this practice by attaching their own trunks so that nobody else could.[11]

Dudley made a concerted effort to remedy the problems of Toby, especially in his column in the *Chicago Defender*, in order to resolve the differences between the box office and backstage and to alleviate the fears of black performers.[12] He suggested that Toby elect a commissioner to arbitrate disputes about salaries, contracts, and problems of low-quality acts. Previously, performers were paid a percentage of the receipts after each engagement. If the house was small, performers could be left with no pay at all. Dudley argued that fixed salaries were better for performers than percentages and schedules should provide acts with consecutive working dates so that "railroad jumps" would be more manageable and salaries more stable. In 1925, in order to improve theater practices and to bolster business for Toby, Dudley wrote:

> Wake up Mr. Actor, and get in right, and Mr. Manager, you who think you can book your house and keep it open playing a company on percentage, your time is limited, so why not let an agent book for you and keep your house open? Of course you can get attractions now and

then but the jumps will kill the actor and sooner or later they will not play for you at all.[13]

By 1926 conditions on Toby had improved. Performers had better living conditions and schedules that permitted them to stay in one area for several weeks instead of constantly "jumping" from one city to another. According to a reporter for the *Pittsburgh Courier*, this allowed them the chance to feel more at home on the road, participate in social activities, and do essential shopping.[14]

Toby had other positive attributes. Although Toby was difficult for small-time performers in terms of compensation and workload, most Toby dancers agreed that the good times they had with other performers made their tenure valuable.[15] Also, headliners such as the Whitman Sisters received traveling expenses, were guaranteed continuous runs, and were almost always treated well. Mabel's skills as a businesswoman were probably still needed, however, to assure that the company was not exploited. Although it was generally easier and more profitable for the Whitman Sisters' company to tour Toby than organize individual bookings as they had in prior years, Mabel still had to look out for shifty theater owners who would try to take advantage of her and the company.

❖ ❖ ❖

An examination of one of the most popular theaters on Toby is useful in analyzing Toby's significance. In New Orleans, during the first two decades of the twentieth century, African Americans were not permitted to attend the performances at the French Opera House, nor were they, regardless of their education or class, given access to the touring symphony concerts and ballets. The Toby-run Lyric Theater was, therefore, the only formal entertainment venue for African Americans in New Orleans. With the responsibility of satisfying all the different aesthetic demands of the African American community in New Orleans, the Lyric Theater had to present opera singers and blackface comedians, classically trained dancers and clowns, blues and jazz music and arias, each form appealing to a different subsection of the audience. Spectators would simply watch what they liked, hold on to their ticket stubs, and wait outside smoking and talking to their friends until something else they liked went on.[16]

The Lyric seated between 350 and 500 people, and as the only venue
for live entertainment for African Americans it was usually full to capacity.
The audience was technically "all-colored," but white spectators did come by
to watch from the balcony the Saturday midnight show (an interesting reversal
of Nigger Heaven). Though unlawful for blacks and whites to be under the
same roof, if the shows were good enough these laws could clearly be
circumvented, and white audiences were able to gain access to these black
shows. As I stated above, a few of the great African American performers chose
not to perform with Toby and preferred touring with white Northern circuits
such as the Keith circuit, if they could get work. The Whitman sisters,
however, decided to stay with Toby, where they could remain the top
attraction and receive the highest salaries. The Whitman Sisters troupe was a
regular feature on the Toby circuit until it diminished in the mid-1930s, and
the company was always able to command top billing. The Whitmans con-
tinually expressed preference for the black theater community while on
Toby.[17] During the 1920s, the Whitman Sisters created at least nine different
shows while touring on Toby. These were: *The Whitman Sisters' Revue* (1923),
Rompin' Through (1924), *Stepping Some* (1924), *Their Gang* (1924), *Goin' Some*
(1925), *Watermelon Morn* (1926), *Miss New York* (1926), *Dancing Fools* (1927), and
Hello Dixieland (1929). *Chicago Defender* reviews of *Rompin' Through* and *Stepping
Some* reaffirm the Whitman Sisters' continued popularity. In a review of *Rompin'
Through*, Tony Langston praised just about every cast member individually in
this "high speed" production in which there was not an idle moment.

> It is a cleverly constructed and perfectly presented entertainment which
> should draw capacity for the full length of the limited engagement. . . .
> It is a great little company and there is justification for saying that never
> before in the history of the Grand has a "tab" aggregation created such
> a sensation.[18]

Speaking of *Stepping Some*, the same reviewer claimed that there were "half a
hundred different things for which it might be recommended to all lovers
of this sort of entertainment."[19]

In 1926, the Whitman Sisters successfully presented *Romping Through*
again at the Howard Theater in Washington, D.C.:

> The Whitman sisters are great favorites in the capital city and have
> always taken well here, but never before has the show packed the
> Howard every show, including matinees to a more satisfied audience,
> that returned the second week equally well satisfied.[20]

While performing *Romping Through* to a standing-room-only crowd at the Howard Theater in Washington D.C., the Whitman sisters met President Coolidge and Mrs. Coolidge, who gave them a tour of the first floor living quarters of the White House. The meeting was arranged by Howard Theater proprietor, Abe Lichtman, manager, E. B. Saunders, and C. Lucien Skinner of the Crispus Attucks Press Association and, undoubtedly, meant good public relations for both the Whitman Sisters and the president. President Coolidge was particularly pleased to meet Princess Wee Wee.

On Toby, the Whitman Sisters continued to mentor some of the best African American performers, including Bill Robinson (who stayed with the troupe from the pre-Toby days), Ma Rainey, and dancers Jack Wiggins, Eddie Rector, Groundhog, and The Berry Brothers. Alice's son, Little Albert "Pops" Whitman, joined the show during this time and remained for ten years until branching off with Louis Williams to form the successful duo Pops and Louis. In a 1924 interview for the *Pittsburgh Courier*, Mabel claimed that as a pioneer, she and other early black performers "paid the price" so that their talented protégés may make it to the legitimate stage. She stated, "If my art hasn't been an inspiration to some ambitious youth, I would rather give it up today."[21]

The serious decline in revenues and activity for many American forms of popular entertainment that began in 1926 intensified after the stock market crash in 1929.[22] The black entertainment forms of musical theater and vaudeville, however, were not as severely damaged as white entertainment forms in the initial impact of the national economic crisis. Despite the difficult times during the 1930s, black musicals in the early part of the Depression did not take the expected decline. In fact, more black musicals and revues appeared in the early 1930s than at any time since the early 1920s. Allen Woll claims several factors protected the black musical from suffering as much as other businesses during the Depression:

> First, these shows were comparatively inexpensive to produce. As black musicals became more and more similar to nightclub presentations in the late 1920s, several expenses were pruned. Out-of-town tryouts were rarely needed, as local clubs from Manhattan to Brooklyn served the purpose. Additionally, the shows did not use much scenery or many costume changes because they concentrated on musical elements.[23]

Also, black actors were given lower wages and were often cast only as "atmosphere" (a status change from "chorus" that permitted wage reductions). After the 1932 season, however, black musicals also started to decline. Along with economic factors, the downturn was due in part to producers who misgauged their audience and relied on formulaic performances that soon tired audiences and critics.

Toby managed to outlast white vaudeville, however.[24] As with black musicals, the troubles of the Depression did not hit black vaudeville until 1932. Ten years earlier, *Billboard* stated that black vaudeville was flourishing in the United States with more than 360 black theaters employing approximately 600 acts. Of these 360 black theaters, 80 of them were affiliated with Toby.[25] In 1929, there were still 80 Toby theaters, but by 1932 most of them were showing only films.

Toby eventually declined and slowly died out during the Depression. Some acts went on to play in white shows, while others, like the Whitman Sisters, worked the independent Negro theaters that remained, theaters such as The Lincoln and the Alhambra in Harlem and later the Apollo. Business-savvy companies like the Whitman Sisters were able to move off Toby when it dissolved, cut costs, incorporate films, and survive the difficult times.

Some sources claim that the Whitman Sisters was breaking up by 1936.[26] Others argue that the breakup began with Mabel's death in 1942, after which the show is said to have struggled for a year, then closed.[27] It was probably the case that the company performed less frequently before the actual breakup, when the sisters began performing extensively outside of the company and when Essie became an evangelist in 1936.

From 1930 to the company's decline during the late 1930s and official breakup in 1943, the Whitman Sisters produced at least six shows, some with Toby and others with independent black houses. The known shows are *Faststeppers* (1930), *Spirit of 1930* (1930), *Wake up Chillun'* (1930), *January Jubilee* (1931), *Step Lively Girls* (1931), and *Swing Revue* (1936).[28] In 1934 Mabel chaperoned Pops and Louis on their tour but the Whitman Sisters would not produce a new show until their last, *Swing Revue*, in 1936. In a 1934 interview, Mabel states, "Some gave the little woman the ha-ha, but we're still here."[29] Mabel planned to keep the name Whitman at the top until her death. She succeeded, though her death came much earlier that she had probably expected.[30] The company struggled to stay active until Mabel's death in 1942 after which the company disbanded for good.

The *Inter-State Tattler* provides a rare review of a later Whitman Sisters show. From it, we learn that the Whitman Sisters remained extremely popular during the 1930s, in part because of the company's abilities to adapt. At the Lafayette theater in Harlem 1931, the company appeared with Bennie Moten's band and the photoplay talkie "The Yellow Ticket," starring John Barrymore's brother, Lionel Barrymore, and the early film actress Elissa Landi in a story about Russia. By adopting the combination format, the sisters could save on costs and offer a "three-in-one" bargain that was well worth the price of admission, even during the Depression. The Whitman sisters stayed loyal to the community by returning to put on a show every year and their audiences, likewise, remained loyal to them. Bennie Butler, reviewer for the *Inter-State Tattler* noted:

> The Whitman Sisters, who make their annual pilgrimage here just like Santa Claus, but never disappoint, have another pleasing musical comedy vehicle. Unlike that old be-whiskered son-of-a-gun, Cris Kringle, they shoot the works every time here and always give of their best. And I wish I could say as much for Santa, who has disappointed me time and time again.[31]

More reliably pleasing than Santa, the Whitman Sisters presented a musical comedy vehicle that lived up to the company's reputation for high-class entertainment by refusing to cut back on the quality of entertainment. Critiquing some of the acts, Butler states:

> A whole show in themselves are Alice and Bert, snappy, clever hoofers who electrify an audience like nobody's business. And what a combination, ye gods? Alice, blonde baby, china doll of syncopation, the peerless dancer, queen of them all. Beautifully formed, charming of mannerisms, she is still the "Baby" Alice to her New York admirers; Bert, the clever masterly impersonator of a hot papa, nattily garbed in masculine wearing apparel, is the ideal beau-brummell. And a flashy dancing partner for the dainty Alice, is the Bert.
>
> Shelton Brooks, superb master of ceremonies, opens the program in his own inimitable way, brimful of witty chatter. Doris Rhembottom, glorious, sweet chirping child of music and mirth, sings her way right into your heart. Eloise Bennett, well known soubrette of Broadway fame, struts her stuff in the well known Bennett way, if you get what I mean. If you don't visit the Lafayette between now and Friday and find out. And Princess Wee Wee that saucy li'l woman, not much bigger that a thumb on your hand, is just too bad, singing and dancing.
>
> Sammy and Scrams, two hoofers, form a novel combination as do the comedy entertainers, Willie Toosweet and "Sparkplug" George. . . .

"Pops" Whitman and Willie (Loonie) Walker, the juvenile steppers know their onions and how to sell 'em and do. Arthur Noble plays a sheik role and twelve pleasing-to-the eye damsels caper about in a way that thrills.[32]

Ernestine Lucas remembers seeing the Whitman Sisters perform in 1931:

When I was a freshman at Fisk University, in 1931-32, the troupe came to Nashville. I was so excited to see them on stage at the Bijou Theatre on Fourth Avenue North. Those were the days when no young lady of refinement went anywhere unescorted. I told my friends about the BIG event that was coming up and we found a senior class girl to be our chaperon. What a time we had![33]

In 1928, the Whitman Sisters bought a new house in Chicago, which became a home base for many traveling African American performers. Although the Whitman sisters had been based in Chicago since 1905, the new house at 425 East Forty-Eighth Street was large enough to put up many traveling black performers who had spent time with the sisters and were always welcome. The Whitman sisters thus continued in their matriarchal roles by providing a safe home for their protégés. In 1928, Princess Wee Wee and another performer known as The Great Thelma both gave their permanent address as 425 East Forty Eighth Street, Chicago, Illinois.[34] It was a place to receive mail (a difficult task for a traveling performer), a place to rest when on the road and a place to call home if need be. The sisters were always looking out for their people, and as the Depression loomed, Essie founded the Theatrical Cheer Club to aid African American performers down on their luck. The Whitmans' neighbor, Mrs. Parham, said that the house was often filled with people. The sisters would give concerts at home. She stated:

Sister Essie, always, always, playing a part, dressed, made up, lots of jewelry and diamonds, and always pleasant, and having great conversations, entertaining with plenty for guests to enjoy of cookies, salads, and dainty pastries [sic].[35]
    They graciouly [sic] served tea and pretty sandwiches, and kept an open door. They had numbers of people around them all the time.[36]

In 1932, the company appeared at the Lincoln Theatre in New Orleans with crowds increasing after each performance. It then toured the West Coast playing California, Oregon, and Washington.[37] Despite the difficult times, this unnamed show prompted one critic to call it "undoubtedly, the greatest edition of the famous Whitman Sisters' many shows."[38]

Between 1935 and 1942, for reasons unknown, the Whitman Sisters performed only sporadically as a company, with each sister branching off at different points. In 1935, after a year hiatus from performing, Alice Whitman danced in *Connie's Hot Chocolates of 1935* at Connie's Inn, marking the first time she performed away from her sisters. The next year, however, she was back with her sisters in *Swing Revue*. This is the last known show the sisters performed together. Mabel was approximately 56, Essie was 54, Alberta was 48, and Alice was 36. Following the close of *Swing Revue*, Alice went on to perform in other New York revues and was a soloist in nightclubs and theaters.

The same year, Caswell Woodfin Whitman, brother of the Whitman Sisters and a musician in his own right, passed away following a lingering illness. He had lived in Atlanta with the family until Reverend Whitman's death and then traveled around the country playing music and making business deals until retiring in 1927 to live with his sisters in Chicago. The obituary stated that the company had split up, with Mabel taking Pops and Louis under the auspices of the NBC radio chain into vaudeville houses, resulting in two trips around the world. Alice spent the year traveling as a single, ending up in Cleveland. The sisters came together to be with each other at the death of their brother and to take the body back to Atlanta to be buried next to their parents; Mabel directed the funeral. Caswell Whitman's obituary pays particular attention to the status of the Whitmans as one of the leading black families in Atlanta.

> The Whitman name means much to people who know of their deeds, which accounts for three of the city's outstanding ministers, Revs. F. D. Jordan, J. P. Evans, and Mrs. Alexander, an evangelist, combining to handle the funeral. Music was furnished by the Metropolitan choir and the Oscar DePriest singers. Mesdames Lucille Thomas and Ruth Powell were soloists on the program.
>
> Among the first of the long list of prominent folk to appear at the residence to pay their respect to the family, were Editor and Mrs. Robert S. Abbott of *The Chicago Defender*. Mr. Abbott, speaking to the family, said he has long felt proud of the Whitman sisters and thought it his duty to come and pay his respects.[39]

In October of the same year, at age 55, Essie decided to leave the stage for the pulpit. She claimed that God had called her three years prior after a miraculous recovery from a auto accident and that since then she had found true happiness. During those three years, Essie worked as an evangelist doing God's work whenever she could between stage engagements.

> God called me after I received an injury to my foot. He told me to go back to my work as an evangelist. You know I was a religious worker when I was 14 years old and before I went on the stage.[40]

Essie continued to remind the world just how religious and respectable the sisters were by telling a *Chicago Defender* reporter that when she was 13 years old she assisted her father in converting 25 people at Hot Springs. She also reminded the reporter that Reverend Whitman was known all over the country as the "Poet Preacher of the World," which served as further testament to the family's respectability. Speaking about her religious influence on stage performers, she proudly stated that Little Pops crossed himself before he did his act. Even in retirement, Essie tried to elevate the status of show business performers by stating that every theatrical performer of any worth or ability was at heart deeply religious.

In 1940, Harry P. Brandon, reporter for the *Philadelphia Tribune,* lamented the state of black entertainment and harshly critiqued Harlem as a home of the stage. "From a most happy condition that stamped it the most fruitful and promising soil for the Negro performer, Harlem has fallen into the place where it is looked upon as the most barren spot in which to plant the seed of hope."[41] The reason given for the decline in African American performance in Harlem was the claim that African American performers relied too heavily on outsiders for support. White booking agents who placed black acts in white and black theaters often took their inflated commissions and invested in white enterprises while caring nothing for the black performers they hired. Clubs that catered to white patrons, such as the famous Cotton Club, were known to mistreat black performers. Brandon considered black performers who were dedicated to entertaining their own people to deserve the most respect, and he was proud to identify the Whitman Sisters as performers loyal to black communities for more than 40 years.

In their final years, the Whitman Sisters continued to entertain black audiences. In a tribute to the Standard Theater, Philadelphia's first vaudeville house, the Whitman Sisters were praised for their contributions:

These beautiful and versatile young women were capable of enacting either individually or in group formation, acts and exhibitions ranging from complete shows to revues, which embraced the charming ingenue and the lady of quality, to the dainty and piquante soubrette and comedienne of the early nineties.[42]

The article showed a picture of Alice and stated that the other members were retired. In 1937, the *New York World Telegram* reported on the talent at the Apollo. Alice Whitman figured prominently in a picture of her and several chorus line girls as they went into a fast number. This picture is an illustration of how a veteran of the Whitman Sisters enthusiastically helped usher in the next generation of African American entertainment for African Americans. She appears with arms akimbo, looking out to the audiences as if to say "Look at what my girls can do!"

"WHITMAN SISTERS' CHAIN IS BROKEN: MABEL IS DEAD"[43]

At 5:30 A.M. on Thursday, May 7, 1942, Mabel Whitman died at Cook County Hospital in Chicago, and her sisters buried her in the family plot at Southview cemetery in Atlanta, Georgia. Working as a theater manager to the end, Mabel had become ill with lobar pneumonia in Detroit several weeks prior, where she was managing and booking her latest pick discoveries, The Four Notes and Santro and Pedro (known as Foster and Prince). When Mabel regained enough strength to travel, Alberta, who had gone to Detroit to be at her bedside, brought her back to the family home in Chicago. Her obituary read:

> The famous chain of Whitman Sisters, known to the American stage as producers and performers for many years, is broken. . . . Mabel Whitman was one of the pioneers of colored show business and for 35 years was the head of the famous Whitman sisters company. She never tired of searching for new talent, and through her interest many of the stars of today owe her a debt of gratitude for giving them their initial start in the theatrical world. She is survived by three sisters, Essie, Alberta and Alice. Pops of the team of Pops and Louie, now playing the Ritz theatre, New York, is also a relative.[44]

"BLAZE KILLS WOMAN, TWO SISTERS ESCAPE"[45]

In May 1963, the Whitman sisters' home on Chicago's Southside, which had served as a refuge and home away from home for so many African American performers, was destroyed by a fire that started in the kitchen and spread throughout the house. Alberta, then age 74, escaped the flames by herself, and Alice, 63, was carried down a ladder to safety by firefighters. But Essie, who was 81 and had been suffering from a heart ailment, was rushed to Provident Hospital after firefighters carried her from the second floor of the house. She died in the hospital of a combination of shock, burns, and smoke inhalation. She is buried in the family plot.

A *Variety* magazine obituary adds:

> A former dancer died Tuesday after firemen rescued her from her burning home at 425 E. 48th [. . .] Firemen said Essie Whitman was terrified as they carried her down the stairs, and the sisters told police she suffered from a heart ailment. She died a short time later.[46]

"3RD OF FAMED WHITMAN SISTERS DIES AT 76"[47]

The following year, Alberta died in Chicago's Cook County Hospital from what was defined only as a prolonged illness. Alice took the body to Atlanta for burial in the family plot. The obituary read:

> Death snuffed out one of the stage's most brilliant lights when it claimed Mrs. Alberta Whitman Bright, 76, one of the famed four Whitman Sisters. . . . The Whitman Sisters skyrocketed to national fame when they operated their traveling revue during the 1920s and 30s. Alberta Whitman was known for her songs, dances and breezy pattern. Often she dressed in male attire, playing opposite her sister, Alice. The Whitman revue played every major vaudeville house in the nation and traveled with a company of 42 persons.[48]

"ALICE WHITMAN OF ONCE FAMOUS WHITMAN SISTERS DIES"[49]

On January 30, 1969, Alice once again joined her sisters. She died of a cerebral hemorrhage in Chicago. She is buried in Lincoln Cemetery, North Township, Illinois. If Alice's short obituary is any indication, we can see in these few lines how the story of these four women was rapidly disappearing from the national consciousness. The obit simply stated that the Whitman Sisters "had a singing and dancing act in the 1920s and toured every vaudeville house in the country. They were discovered as they sang jubilee songs at a church concert by agents who thought they were white."[50]

In March 1954, *Ebony* magazine ran a piece comparing contemporaneous black beauties with those of the past. With the Whitman sisters' many accomplishments managing and performing on the vaudeville stage for more than 40 years, it is unfortunate that one of the last extant articles on the sisters focused solely on their physical appearance. The article reveals much about the gender politics of the 1920s through the 1950s and the standards by which America had valued black female performers. The piece focused on Negro show business during the early part of the century, particularly the role of the dancing girls in shows like *The Smart Set, Brownskin Models,* and *Bandanna Days.* The Whitman Sisters were acclaimed for their light-skinned beauty without mention of the fact that their chorus lines featured many different types, as they challenged the light-skinned beauty standard. This example proves how the issues of colorism and beauty that were in operation during the Whitman Sisters' heyday were still influential in the 1950s. They are still with us today.

The only other time the Whitman Sisters are named in a mainstream periodical is a small mention in a 1977 *New York Times* article about a museum exhibit on blacks in theater that simply stated the Whitman Sisters was one of the most popular acts booked by Toby. This is the first time the Whitman Sisters had ever been mentioned in this prestigious white newspaper.

In 1999, Ronald "Smokey" Stevens and Jaye Stewart wrote the musical *Rollin' on the T.O.B.A.,* a fictional account of three performers on the early Negro vaudeville circuit. Performing with the Whitman Sisters is mentioned as the making the big-time.

According to Ernestine Lucas, there are no surviving Whitmans: "Male offsprings of the mulatto Whitman family with the Whitman name are nonexistent [*sic*]. . . . There is no one to carry on the family name."[51]

I wanted to end the book with the last primary documentation of the Whitman Sisters and the mark they left on vaudeville, but it is clear that the importance of their work extends far beyond this brief mention. The last few reports of the Whitman Sisters' work in the press offer sadly inadequate coverage of the group's contribution to American theater and dance. But through this book, we are able to more fully grasp the place of the Whitman Sisters in theater history. Writing the Whitmans back into history allows us to see the range of negotiations that were necessary for a black company to succeed in the American vaudeville industry. Performers like the Whitmans had to carefully control the images they portrayed in order to stay in the "big time." From the time they performed in front of their first audiences, singing and dancing on their father's evangelical tour, through their years as an independent troupe playing the top vaudeville houses and their time as headliners on Toby to the end of their 40-year careers, Mabel, Alberta, Essie, and Alice made sure that they and their company of performers had a variety of top-rate acts, were never taken advantage of, and maintained spotless reputations. Because they were so popular and well respected, they were able to take certain liberties in their portrayal of African American female identity by challenging the fictions of race and gender. Ever loyal to the African American community, especially the black church, the Whitman Sisters entertained whites and blacks, men and women, upper-, middle-, and lower-class Americans. They trained many of the subsequent generation of African American performers (see appendix list of performers who worked with the Whitman Sisters) and carved a niche for themselves in the theater world as the Royalty of Negro Vaudeville.

Perhaps conclusion is the wrong word for the end of this book because in many ways I want to show how this work is a beginning. There are many other avenues beyond the scope of this text that need to be explored. As I mentioned, many major figures in African American performance received their training from the Whitman Sisters. Work that traced the influences of early African American performers on later generations would be invaluable to the field. A full-length study of the importance of the Theatre Owners' Booking Association as the major black vaudeville circuit and its impact on early twentieth-century society needs to be pursued. And certainly, more work could be done on the role music played in early black performances.

I also envision an in-depth piece looking at African American performance in terms of geography. How did performances differ between city and rural areas, the North and the South, the East and the West? How did the Great Migration impact African American theater? Why did some performers choose to perform as small-time acts on white circuits rather than headliners on Toby? Was Southern racism the only reason? How did African American performance contribute to the cultural formation of different cities at the beginning of the nineteenth century as well as the westward expansion? What were the similarities and difference between the United States and other countries in terms of how black performers were treated and how black performances were received? What were the social politics of touring?

Also interesting would be a detailed study of the sociopolitical ramifications of the rhetoric of "yours" and "ours." How did the desire to promote positive images of African American representatives influence social and economic policy? How did the history of African American criticism shift over time in light of different political agendas? What were the differences between reviews of performances in small towns versus those in big cities? What else can be said about the differences and similarities between white and black reviewers?

And of course more recuperative analytical histories of early African American theater and dance personalities must be done. There are many more stories to be told. Only when we tell them will a complete picture of this period of American theater history be drawn and only then will we understand and appreciate the legacy these people left us. I think Mabel said it well:

> There are few who can appreciate the wonderful progress our group has made on the legitimate stage. Only those who have had something to do with the pioneer work realize the task it has been to make good. Today the average girl of talent and personality can "go over" in a night. I wonder if we who have done the foundation work are not responsible for a greater day for the Negro stage artist? If so, I am happy.[52]

Chronology

June 1875—Caswell Whitman, brother to the Whitman sisters born in Xenia, OH.

May 1880—Mabel Whitman is born in either Lawrence, KS or Van Wert, OH.

July 4, 1882—Essie Barbara Whitman is born in Oseceola, AR.

ca. 1887—Alberta Whitman is born in Pratt, KS.

ca. 1890s—The sisters begin performing with Rev. A. A. Whitman in Kansas City, MO.

ca. 1899—Mabel and Essie begin singing professionally.

May 1, 1899—The Whitman Sisters' Comedy Co. plays Savannah, GA, theaters to both white and black audiences.

ca. 1900—Alice Whitman is born, probably in Atlanta, GA.

ca. 1900—The Whitman Sisters Comedy Co. plays Augusta Grand Opera House, Augusta, GA; Burbridge's Opera House in Jacksonville, FL, and Savannah Theatre in Savannah, GA. They then tour all of the leading Southern houses.

June 29, 1901—The Reverend Albery Allson Whitman dies.

February 22, 1902—The Whitman Sisters' Novelty Co. opens midwinter at the Grand Opera House, Augusta, GA.

July 11 through July 23, 1904—The Whitman Sisters' New Orleans Troubadours plays at the Jefferson Theatre, Birmingham, AL.

December 10, 1904—The Whitman Sisters Concert Co. tours Kentucky.

ca. 1905—The Whitman Sisters Concert Co. moves its base of operations to Chicago, IL.

March 4, 1905—The Whitman Sisters Concert Co. tours Arkansas.

October 14, 1905—For four weeks, the Whitman Sisters Concert Co. tours the leading churches in St. Louis, MO.

ca. 1906—Will Marion Cook places the Whitman Sisters on a program of a private musicale held in honor of a Judge Gray at the Waldorf Astoria in New York.

May 1, 1906—The Whitman Sisters plays at the Palm Gardens.

October 8, 1906—The Whitman Sisters plays in Worcester, MA.

January 1, 1907—The Whitman Sisters plays in Lowell, MA.

May 9, 1908—The Whitman Sisters plays Washington, D.C. at the Second Baptist Church.

May 11 through June 11, 1908—The Whitman Sisters plays the following D.C. churches for one month:

>   Ebenezer A. M. E. Church, Monday, May 11, 1908.
>
>   Friendship Church, Friday, May 15.
>
>   Return engagement, Second Baptist Church, Monday, May 18.
>
>   Mt. Airy Baptist Church, Tuesday, May 19.
>
>   Vermost Avenue Baptist Church, Wednesday, May 20.
>
>   Trinity A. M. E. Church, Thursday, May 21.
>
>   Tenth Street Baptist Church, Friday, May 22.
>
>   Metropolitan A. M. E. Church, Monday, May 25.
>
>   St. Paul A. M. E. Church, Tuesday, May 26.
>
>   Lane C. M. E. Church, Wednesday, May 27.
>
>   Walker Memorial Baptist Church, Thursday, May 28.

Return to Ebenezer A. M. E. Church, Friday, May 29.

Metropolitan Baptist Church, Monday, June 1.

Ebenezer A. M. E. Church, Wednesday, June 3.

Cosmopolitan Temple Baptist Church, Thursday, June 11.

December 26, 1908—The Whitman Sisters plays in San Jose, CA.

ca. 1909—Al Sutherland signs the Whitman Sisters to the Pantages circuit.

May 8, 1909—Caddie Whitman (mother) dies in Atlanta, GA. Funeral at Big Bethel A. M. E. Church in Atlanta.

ca. 1910—Alice Whitman joins the company. (By this time the sisters played most of the major vaudeville circuits in the South, East, and Northeast.)

January 2 through January 29, 1910—The Whitman Sisters plays at Lagman's Theatre, Mobile, AL.

February 12, 1910—The Whitman Sisters and Billy Kersands' vaudeville company play Lagman's Theatre, Mobile, AL.

June 4, 1910—The Whitman Sisters plays a five-week engagement at the Colored Air Dome Theatre, Jacksonville, FL.

October 15, 1910—The Whitman Sisters plays Atlanta, GA, for three weeks.

November 26, 1910—The Whitman Sisters performs at Swords Theatre, Chattanooga, TN.

1910—The company tours with a show titled "The Whitman Sisters Review."

1911–1913—The sisters split up briefly between 1911 and 1913, with Alice leaving the show temporarily, Mabel doing a single act in Southern houses, and Essie and Alberta forming a small vaudeville group that plays throughout the East.

1914—The sisters are again united and work independently of a circuit. A small company that includes two picks known as Aaron and Sambo joins the Whitman Sisters. The new larger company is featured on the Family United circuit and spends about 20 weeks in and around Boston.

November 30, 1914—The Whitman Sisters plays Boston Theatre in Lynchburg, VA, with the S. H. Dudley Circuit.

December 25, 1915—The Whitman Sisters plays in Cincinnati at the Lincoln.

1916—The Whitman Sisters produces and performs "The Black Coachman."

January 26, 1918—The Whitman Sisters performs at the Owl Theater in Chicago.

ca. 1920s—The Whitman Sisters joins TOBA (Toby).

October 16, 1920—Alberta Whitman writes the song "Think of Me, Little Daddy," which is published by Pace and Handy Music Co. Inc.

1924—The Whitman Sisters produces and performs "Rompin' Through" and "Their Gang."

1925—The Whitman Sisters produces and performs "Going Some."

1926—The Whitman Sisters produces and performs "Going Some," "Rompin' Through," "Watermelon Morn," and "Miss New York."

1927—The Whitman Sisters produces and performs "Dancing Fools."

1928—The Whitman Sisters company is booked for a year run on the Publix Circuit.

1928—The Whitman sisters buy a home in Chicago.

January 19, 1929—Alice Whitman dances at the Royal Theatre for a week.

1929—The Whitman Sisters produces and performs "Hello Dixieland."

1929—The Whitman Sisters performs at the 81 Theater in Atlanta, GA.

1930—The Whitman Sisters produces and performs "Faststeppers," "Spirit of 1930," and "Wake Up Chillun'."

1931—The Whitman Sisters produces and performs "January Jubilee," and "Step Lively Girls."

1931—The Whitman Sisters and Moten's Band play at the Lafayette Theater in NYC.

December 1931—The Whitman Sisters performs at the Howard Theater in Washington, D.C.

December 17, 1932—The Whitman Sisters plays the Lincoln Theatre in New Orleans, LA, for two weeks and then tour Southwest to California, Oregon, and Washington.

April 27, 1935—Alice Whitman performs in "Connie's Hot Chocolates of 1935" at Connie's Inn in NYC.

1936—The Whitman Sisters produces and performs "Swing Revue."

April 4, 1936—Caswell Woodfin Whitman, brother of the Whitman sisters, and one of the country's leading musicians, dies in Chicago, IL.

October 3, 1936—Essie Whitman stops performing to become an evangelist.

January 23, 1937—Alice Whitman performs in "Harlem Stompers" at the Apollo in NYC.

May 7, 1942—Mabel Whitman (62?) dies in Chicago, IL.

May 7, 1963—Essie Barbara Whitman (81) dies in Chicago, IL.

June 27, 1964—Alberta Whitman (76) dies in Chicago, IL.

January 30, 1969—Alice Whitman (68?) dies in Chicago, IL.

February 11, 1977—The Whitman sisters are recognized in a New York exhibit, "Dixie to Broadway."

The following is a list of people known to have worked
with the Whitman Sisters:

NAME	ROLE
Aaron and Sammy	picks
Accooe, Will	music director
Adams, Billy	pick
Allman, Alfreda	dancer
Anderson, Archie	violinist
Anderson, Charles	singer, yodeler
Anderson, Eddie (Rochester)	comedian
Anthony, Emmett	comedian
Babero, Arnett	singer and dancer
Basie, Catherine	dancer
Basie, William (Count)	musician
Bennett, Eloise	singer
Bernhardt, Clyde	trombonist
Berry, Ananias and Jimmy	dancers
Bones, Shine	performer
Bow, Mike	blackface comedian
Bradley, Linwood	drummer
Brandon, Willie	performer
Briggs, Bunny	pick tap dancer
Bright, Lois	dancer
Brooks, Shelton	master of ceremonies
Brown, Mary E.	dancer
Bryant, Willie	comedian

Butterbeans and Susie	comedians
Calloway, Harriet	dancer
Carrol, Albert	music director
Carter, Paul (Too Sweet)	performer
Campbell, Dick	performer
Chapman, Pearl	performer
Chimebones	pick tap dancer
Clark, Raymond	performer
Claybrook, Bob	cornetist
Coleman, Gladys	dancer
Creole Mike	performer
Curry, Leona	singer
Cut-Out	performer
Davis, George M.	music trainer
DeGaston, Gallie	singer and recitation
Dorsey, Mattie	singer
Douglass, Katie	performer
Durand, Billy	performer
Earthquake, Billy	comedian
Edgeson, Lawrence C.	trombonist
Edwards, B. E.	tenor soloist
Ellis, Bernice Olivia	singer
Evans, Billie	singer
Feribee, Elsie	performer
Fisher, Kite	performer
Five Spirits Of Rhythm (Ben Bernie's Nephews)	band
Fleming, Moses	temporary business manager
Floyd, Josephine	dancer
Fortune, Myrtle	dancer
Foxworth, Julius	picks
Franklin, Katie	performer

Frye, Ethel	dancer
Gay, Annie	performer
George, Bernice	dancer
George, Sparkplug	comedian
Gilbert, Lou	performer
Gomez, Inez	performer
Grant, Tony	performer
Green, Buddle	comedian
Gulfport and Brown	picks
Haines, Christine	dancer
Hamilton, Mr. and Mrs.	performers
Harris, Toy	performer
Harris and Holly	comedians
Hawkins, Thomas Wellington	pick
Hayes, Florence	dancer
Henderson, Slim	comedian and stage manager
Hubert, Joe	emcee and performer
Jackson, Tony	comedian, pianist, singer
Jazzlips, Little	pick
Jenkins, Sammy	performer
Johnson, Lonnie	band leader
Johnson, Walter B.	performer
Jones, Charley	performer
Jones, Joe	dancer
Kersands, Billy	singer, dancer, comedian
Kersands, Louise	assistant to Billy Kersands
King, Billy	comedian
Kyle, Bobbie	performer
La Alberta, Bastiste	performer
Langston, Dorothy	saxophonist
LaRue, John	comedian
LeGon, Jeni	dancer

Loften, William	comedian
Mabley, Jackie "Moms"	comedienne
Madison, Rastus Airship	comedian
McClennon, Frank	performer
McCree, Maxie	pick, Alberta's husband
McCurdy, Dolly	dancer
Michaels, Ernest	performer
Mills, Billy	comedian
Mitchell, Billy	pick
Moten, Bennie	composer
Murphy, Jeanette	performer
Nash, Ruth	dancer
Nelson, Daybreak	comedian
Noble, Arthur	performer
Oliver, Josephine	performer
Orman, Elfreda	performer
Palmer, Aaron	pick, Alice's husband
Payne, Delores	dancer
Payne, Sterling	alto sax
Payton, Dave	tutor, Mabel's husband
Peyton, Frank	temporary business manager
Pops and Dotty	performers
Price, Annie Mae	singer
Princess Wee Wee	performer
Rainey, Ma	singer
Rector, Eddie	dancer
Redeaus, Clifford	saxophonist
Reed, Sambo	comedian
Rhembottom, Doris	singer
Rhodes, Cliff	contortionist
Ricks, Ida Mae	dancer
Robinson, Willie	dancer

Rogers, James	performer
Sammy and Scrams	picks
Santro and Pedro	
(Foster and Prince)	picks
Show Boy	performer
Smith, Clarence "Pinetop"	pianist
Smith, Lulu	performer
Smith, Shirrod	saxophonist and vocalist
Smith, Walter	trap drummer
Snapp, Troy	pianist and director of the Chicago Night Hawks orchestra
Straighter, Zelma	performer
Struffin, Gertrude	dancer
Tapp, Ferman	comedian
Taylor, Bessie	performer
Taylor, Clarence (Groundhog)	pick
The Five OK Boys	picks
The Four Cotton Pickers	picks
The Four Notes	picks
Thomas, Eugene	singer
Thompson, Vivian	toe dancer
Too Sweet, Lulu	performer
Too Sweet, Willie	blackface comedian
Towels, Leslie J.	drummer
Travis, Alma	dancer
Walker, Willie (Loonie)	dancer
Walker, Bootsie	dancer
Washington, Dorothy	performer
Washington, Miles	performer
Waters, Ethel	singer
Watkins, Margaret	singer

Watson, Leo	jazz singer
Whitman, Jessie (adopted sister)	performer
Whitman, Little Albert (Pops)	dancer
Whitman, Mattie (adopted sister)	performer
Whitman, Pat (adopted sister)	dancer
Whitman, Ruth (adopted sister)	dancer
Wiggins, Jack	dancer
Williams, Mary Lou	composer-pianist
Willis, Ethel	dancer
Wilson, Marbel	dancer
Yates, Billie	performer

Toby Theaters

A list of Toby theaters and managers is provided in
The 1928 Official Theatrical World of Colored Artists. They include:

LOCATION	THEATER	MANAGER
Asheville, NC	Eagle	Harry Roth
Atlanta, GA	Eighty-one	Tom Baily
Austin, TX	Lyric	E. H. Givens
Baltimore, MD	Regal	Various
Baton Rouge, LA	Grand	Ernest Boehringer
Beaumont, TX	Joland	Lawrence Fontana
Bessemer, AL	Frolic	Ben Jaffee
Birmingham, AL	Frolic	H. J. Hury
Charlotte, NC	Rex	S. W. Craver
Chattanooga, TN	Liberty	Sam E. Reevin
Chicago, IL	Grand	H. B. Miller
Chicago, IL	Monogram	H. B. Miller
Cincinnati, OH	Roosevelt	Jack Lustgarten
Cleveland, OH	Globe	M. B. Horwitz
Columbia, SC	Royal	Earl Pinkerton
Columbus, OH	Pythian	Henry F. Eger
Dallas, TX	Ella B. Moore	Chintz Moore
Dayton, OH	Palace	Lloyd H. Cox

Detroit, MI	Koppin	H. S. Koppin
Durham, NC	Wonderland	G. W. Logan
East St. Louis, IL	Lincoln	Harry Hershenson
Ensley, AL	Palace	R. V. Rhinehart
Galveston, TX	Rialto	A. Martini
Gary, IN	Broadway	G. B. Young
Greensboro, NC	Palace	Charles Roth
Hot Springs, AR	Gem Theatre	Stanley Lee
Houston, TX	American	Paul Barracco
Houston, TX	Washington	Paul Barracco
Jackson, TN	Gem	E. L. Drake
Kansas City, MO	Lincoln	Rubin Finklestein
Knoxville, TN	Gem	M. C. Kennedy
Louisville, KY	Lincoln	J. A. C. Lattimore
Macon, GA	Douglass	Ben Stein
Memphis, TN	Palace	A. Barrasso
Mobile, AL	Pike	C. B. King
Nashville, TN	Bijou	Milton Starr
Newbern, NC	Globe	E. L. Lewis
Oklahoma City, OK	Aldrige	Zelia N. Breaux
Pittsburgh, PA	Elmore	Ben Engleberg
Port Arthur, TX	Dreamland	Lawrence Fontana
Shreveport, LA	Star	Arthur Cunningham
Springfield, OH	Booker Washington	S. C. Olinger
Springfield, OH	Lincoln	J. W. Hamilton
St. Louis, MO	Booker Washington	Charles H. Turpin
Tulsa, OK	Dreamland	W. M. Cherry
Waco, TX	Gaiety	J. A. Lemke
Washington, DC	Howard	Various
Wilmington, NC	Brooklyn	Robert Herring
Winston-Salem, NC	Lincoln	W. S. Scales

Notes

PREFACE: SURVIVING THE SILENCE

1. Marshall Stearns and Jean Stearns, *Jazz Dance: The Story of American Vernacular Dance* (New York: Da Capo Press, 1994), 89.

2. Rosalyn Terborg-Penn, "Discontented Black Feminist." In *We Specialize in the Wholly Impossible: A Reader in Black Women's History*, ed. Darlene Clark Hine et al. (Brooklyn: Carlson, 1995), 487-503.

3. Many contemporary feminist scholars are taking steps to recognize these complexities, but as Higginbotham explains, the problems persist. For a good introduction to the discussion of the history of feminism and race one may want to begin with Evelyn Brooks Higginbotham, "African-American Women's History and the Metalanguage of Race," in *We Specialize in the Wholly Impossible*, 3.

4. Paula Giddings, *When and Where I Enter: The Impact of Black Women on Race and Sex in America* (New York: Bantam Books, 1984), 311. For further discussion of black chauvinism during the 1960s and black women's reaction read this text from pages 311-324.

5. Angela Davis, *Angela Davis: An Autobiography* (New York: Random House, 1974), 161.

6. *New Minstrel and Black Face Joke Book by Leading Footlight Favorites* (Baltimore: Ottenheimer, 1907), 33.

7. Glenda Dickerson, "The Cult of True Womanhood: Toward a Womanist Attitude in African-American Theatre." In *Performing Feminisms: Feminist Critical Theory and Theatre*, ed. Sue Ellen Case (Baltimore: Johns Hopkins UP, 1990), 110.

8. Hazel V. Carby, Reconstructing Womanhood: The Emergence of the Afro-American Woman Novelist (New York: Oxford UP, 1987), 6.

9. Maria Stewart, "Productions of Mrs. Maria W. Stewart." In *Daughters of Africa: An International Anthology of Words and Writings by Women of African Descent from the Ancient Egyptian to the Present*, ed. Margaret Busby (New York: Ballantine Books, 1992), 47.

10. Audre Lorde, *Sister Outsider: Essays and Speeches* (Freedom, CA: The Crossing Press Feminist Series, 1984), 44.

11. bell hooks, *Talking Back: Thinking Feminist, Thinking Black* (Boston: South End Press, 1989), 9.

12.   Maya Angelou, *I Know Why The Caged Bird Sings* (New York: Bantam Books, 1969), 231.

13.   Anna Julia Cooper first used this phrase in 1892 to refer to the success of the struggles of the African American race occurring when the black woman is accepted with dignity and without violence. We will be able to measure the success by the entrance of the African American woman. Paula Giddings also evokes this term when writing the history of African American women. I use the term here to explain the participation of the black female scholar in the struggles against oppression. Of course, the complexities of oppression and exclusion extend far beyond African American women's plight for equality.

14.   See VèVè A. Clark, "The Archaeology of Black Theatre," *The Black Scholar* 10.10 (July/August 1979): 43-56.

15.   Alice Walker, *In Search of Our Mothers' Gardens: Womanist Prose* (New York: Harcourt Brace and Company, 1984), 93-116.

16.   Stearns 91.

17.   Adrienne Rich discusses the problems of attempting to speak for someone else in "Notes Toward a Politics of Location," in her book *Women, Feminist Identity, and Society in the 1980s* (Philadelphia: Benjamins, 1985), 16.

CHAPTER 1: INTRODUCTION

1.   Samuel A. Hay, *African American Theatre: An Historical and Critical Analysis* (New York: Cambridge UP, 1994).

2.   Edward Thorpe, *Black Dance* (Woodstock, NY: Overlook Press, 1990).

3.   For example, there is no mention of the Whitman Sisters in the following texts on black theater and dance: Allen Woll, *Black Musical Theatre: From Coontown to Dreamgirls* (New York: Da Capo Press, 1989); Errol Hill, ed., *The Theatre of Black Americans: A Collection of Critical Essays* (New York: Applause, 1987); Richard A. Long, *Black Dance: The Black Tradition in American Modern Dance* (New York: Rizzoli, 1989); Lynne Fauley Emery, *Black Dance: From 1619 to Today* (Princeton, NJ: Princeton Book Company, 1988).

4.   For a discussion of the relationship between the Harlem Renaissance and folk culture see the following texts: Alain Locke, *The New Negro: Voices of the Harlem Renaissance* (New York: Atheneum, 1992); Jervis Anderson, *This Was Harlem* (New York: Noonday Press, 1982); Nathan Irvin Huggins, *Harlem Renaissance* (New York: Oxford UP, 1971); David Levering Lewis, *When Harlem Was in Vogue* (New York: Oxford UP, 1981); and Margaret Just Butcher, *The Negro in American Culture* (New York: Alfred A. Knopf, 1972).

5. Lawrence Levine examines the meaning of folk culture in *Black Culture and Black Consciousness: Afro-American Folk Thought from Slavery to Freedom* (New York: Oxford UP, 1977).

6. James V. Hatch, "Here Comes Everybody: Scholarship and Black Theater History." In *Interpreting the Theatrical Past*, ed. Thomas Postlewait and Bruce A. McConachie (Iowa City: University of Iowa Press, 1989), 148.

7. Robert L. Johns, "The Whitman Sisters." In *Notable Black Women, Book II*, ed. Jessie Carney Smith (New York: Gale Research, 1996), 707.

8. Johns 707.

9. For a discussion of Bert Williams and the image of the African American male performer during the early twentieth century, see Sandra L. Richards, "Bert Williams: The Man and The Mask," *Mime, Mask & Marionette* 101 (Spring 1978): 6-25. For a discussion of Bert Williams and the ways in which he confronted racism, see Blanche Ferguson, "Black Skin, Black Mask: The Inconvenient Grace of Bert Williams," *American Visions* 7:3 (June/July 1992): 14-18.

10. Woll argues that Williams' move to the white world of musical comedy sent a devastating blow to the already declining black musical theater business. The pros and cons of these decisions are clear, and Williams' choice to move to the Follies, like the Whitman Sisters' choice to play primarily to black audiences, can be seen as an important, albeit complicated, step for African Americans.

11. Woll, 46.

12. For example, in "Bert Williams: The Man and The Mask," 15-16, Sandra L. Richards points to the reviewers of the singing, dancing, and joke-telling trio of Bert Williams, George Walker, and Ada Walker, who lamented and were angered by the performers' attempts to move beyond stereotypes and present refinement. Also, in *Black Musical Theatre*, Allen Woll discusses critical reaction to the Cole and Johnson play *The Shoo-Fly Regiment*. The critic for *Theatre* gave the show a bad review for not using stereotypes and for being too close to white productions.

13. To compare reviews of early black performances one may want to begin with Henry T. Sampson's *The Ghost Walks: A Chronological History of Blacks in Show Business, 1865-1910*. (Metuchen, NJ: Scarecrow Press, 1988). Within this chronology are reprints of many reviews. It is clear that the reviews in white papers are typically brief compared to those in black papers.

14. For example see André Levinson, "The Negro Dance Under European Eyes," *Theatre Arts* (April 1927): 282-293.

15. Levinson.

16. For several examples of the popularity of black folk tradition during the 1920s see Alain Locke's *The New Negro*.

17. *The New York Tribune*, October 28, 1871.

18. For a good introduction to these methodologies see Patricia Hill Collins, *Black Feminist Thought: Knowledge, Consciousness, and the Politics of Empowerment* (New York: Routledge, 1991), and Angela Davis, *Women, Race and Class* (New York: Vintage Books, 1981).

19. Alice Walker, *In Search of our Mothers' Gardens: Womanist Prose* (New York: Harcourt Brace and Company, 1984), xi. As I am also committed to the wholeness of entire people, this book is not separatist in intent and is intended for everyone interested in investigating the intricacies of race, class, and gender in operation in black vaudeville.

20. Patricia Hill Collins, *Black Feminist Thought*, 39.

21. Collins, 15.

22. Barbara Christian, "The Race for Theory," *Feminist Studies* 14.1 (Spring 1988): 75.

23. This is a major issue in feminist theory as a whole. Adrienne Rich points to the exclusionary practices of white feminist theory and the complexities of oppression in "Notes Toward a Politics of Location," *Women, Feminist Identity, and Society in the 1980s* (Philadelphia: Benjamins, 1985). See also Sue Ellen Case, *Feminism and Theatre* (New York: Routledge, 1988), 95; and Gayle Austin, *Feminist Theories for Dramatic Criticism* (Ann Arbor: University of Michigan Press, 1990), 7.

24. Evelyn Brooks Higginbotham, "African-American Women's History and the Metalanguage of Race." In *We Specialize in the Wholly Impossible: A Reader in Black Women's History*, ed. Darlene Clark Hine, et al. (New York: Carlson, 1995).

25. Higginbotham discusses this strategy of borrowing and blending methodologies in "African-American Women's History and the Metalanguage of Race," 4.

26. Elaine Aston, *An Introduction to Feminism and Theatre* (New York: Routledge, 1995), 15-16.

27. VèVè Clark, "The Archaeology of Black Theatre," *The Black Scholar* 10.10 (1979): 43-56.

28. Carter G. Woodson, *The Mis-Education of the Negro* (London: African World Press, 1990), 21.

29. Lawrence W. Levine, *Highbrow/Lowbrow: The Emergence of Cultural Hierarchy in America* (Cambridge, MA: Harvard UP, 1988).

CHAPTER 2: SETTING THE STAGE

1. *The Washington Bee*, May 23, 1908.

2. According to the 1900 Atlanta census, Essie, Mabel, and their brother Caswell also worked as music teachers. Alberta was in school.

3. For interesting discussions of entertainment in Atlanta see: Herman Mason, *African-American Entertainment in Atlanta* (Atlanta: Arcadia, 1998), Clifford M. Kuhn, et al., *Living Atlanta: An Oral History of the City, 1914-1948* (Atlanta: The University of Georgia Press, 1990), and Michael Leroy Porter, *Black Atlanta: An Interdisciplinary Study of Blacks of the East Side of Atlanta, 1890-1930* (Emory University Dissertation, 1974).

4. Jubilees are African American religious songs usually referring to a time of future happiness or jubilation.

5. Henry T. Sampson, *The Ghost Walks: A Chronological History of Blacks in Show Business, 1865-1910* (Metuchen, NJ: Scarecrow Press, 1988).

6. As I discuss in detail later, the sisters would keep their ties to the church and their respectable images throughout their careers.

7. Higginbotham, *Righteous Discontent: The Women's Movement in the Black Baptist Church, 1880-1920* (Cambridge, MA: Harvard University Press, 1993), 6.

8. I discuss these strategies in greater detail in the next chapter.

9. The popular "Sometimes I Feel Like a Motherless Child" is a good example of a sorrow song. See James Weldon Johnson, *The Book of American Negro Spirituals* (New York: Viking Press, 1925) for other examples.

10. Langston Hughes and Milton Meltzer, *Black Magic: A Pictorial History of the African-American in the Performing Arts* (New York: Da Capo Press, 1967) 126.

11. Hatch, 153.

12. Hatch, 153.

13. Sampson, 6.

14. "He's Got the Whole World in His Hands" is a good example of a jubilee song.

15. Perry Bradford, *Born With The Blues* (New York: Oak, 1965) 19.

16. Bill Reed speculates that the young "Georgia Tom" Dorsey may have drawn some of the inspiration for his jazz + spirituals = gospel experiments like "Peace in the Valley" and "Precious Lord, Take my Hand" from the music of the Whitman Sisters. Since he was born in the Whitman's home state, he may have had the opportunity to see them perform. See Bill Reed, *"Hot From Harlem": Profiles in Classic African-American Entertainment* (Los Angeles: Cellar Door Books, 1998) 35.

17. Several sources cite this phrase, which was undoubtedly used for promotional purposes. The "record" mentioned is never specified and may or may not be official. It is not extant at this time, however.

18. The four sisters later attended the New England Conservatory of Music in Boston, Massachusetts, for five years under the personal training of the instructor George M. Davis and later studied at Morris Brown College in Atlanta, Georgia where their father served as dean.

19. Henry T. Sampson, *Blacks in Blackface: A Source Book On Early Black Musical Shows* (Metuchen, NJ: Scarecrow Press, 1980), 101. Mabel and Essie may have chosen the name Danzette for the security provided by using a pseudonym. Several performers changed their names, especially if an act was unsuccessful. One could always move to another city and open up a new act with a new name.

20. Caddie Whitman was also known as Kate, Katie, and Cad. Records on her life are scarce. She was born ca. 1857 in Kentucky.

21. "The Whitmans," *Chicago Defender*, January 26, 1918.

22. According to another account, which appeared on page 57 of the March 1954 *Ebony*, white audiences "discovered" the Whitman Sisters long after they had been entertaining black audiences, when British nobility out "slumming" in New York's Negro district around Fifty-Third Street heard Mabel, Alberta, and Essie singing jubilee songs at the Metropolitan Baptist Church.

23. *The Indianapolis Freeman*, February 6, 1897.

24. Ernestine Garrett Lucas, *Wider Windows to the Past: African American History from a Family Perspective* (Decorah, Iowa: Anundsen, 1995)

25. See Sampson, 367.

26. Two of the most famous African American expatriate performers were Ira Aldridge and Josephine Baker. For more information on their careers one might begin by reading Herbert Marshall and Mildred Stock's book *Ira Aldridge: Negro Tragedian* (Washington, D.C.: Howard UP, 1993), and Josephine Baker's autobiography, *Josephine* by Josephine Baker and Jo Bouillon (New York: Paragon House, 1988).

27. I will further probe the theoretical implications of popular performance and the politics of respectability on the Whitmans' touring policies in the next chapter.

28. For programs of black vaudeville performances and to track the practices of the Hyer Sisters and Sissieretta Jones see Henry T. Sampson's, *The Ghost Walks*

29. Reed, 33.

30. Clarence Muse was also a performer at this time. His book *Way Down South* is a manuscript in scrapbook form in which Muse gossips about others in show business. All citations from him used in this book must be read with a degree of suspicion as he does not support his claims with evidence. To omit them completely would be irresponsible, however.

31. Clarence Muse and David Arlen, *Way Down South* (Hollywood, CA: David Graham Fischer, 1932).

32. We do not know if Caddie was still chaperoning the girls at this time, or Reverend Whitman's feelings toward her, but there is no evidence to suggest that the two were divorced or estranged.

33. *The Birmingham News,* February 22, 1902.

34. Reed, 233n16, and personal interview, December 7, 1999.

35. Quoted in Reed 36.

36. *The Washington Bee,* May 30, 1908

37. *The Washington Bee,* May 30, 1908

38. I discuss black female respectability further in the next chapter.

39. Joan R. Sherman, "Albery Allson Whitman: Poet of Beauty and Manliness," *CLA Journal* 1 (November 1957): 127.

40. Joan R. Sherman, *African-American Poetry of the Nineteenth Century* (Chicago: University of Illinois Press, 1992), 236.

41. Ernestine Lucas has written a family history for the Lucas and Garrett families. It is a well-researched and lovingly crafted tribute to her family. The Whitmans are an important part of this family history. The sections on the Whitman family extend back to slavery and include a discussion of the slave family that owned the Whitmans. Interestingly, the family permitted pictures of their slaves with books in their hands. This was unusual since teaching slaves to read was illegal. It is also known family lore that Albery Whitman could read from the time he was three years old. His poems provide many of the clues Ernestine Lucas used to trace the Whitman family line. For more biographical information on Reverend Whitman and other Whitman ancestors, including a poem written by Reverend Whitman in memory of his mother, see Ernestine Garrett Lucas, *Wider Windows to the Past: African American History from a Family Perspective* (Decorah, Iowa: Anundsen, 1995).

42. Joan R. Sherman, "Albery Allson Whitman: Poet of Beauty and Manliness," 127.

43. Essie Whitman made this claim. See Stearns 85. Ernestine Lucas claims this was a family joke and the sisters were just trading on the name to get attention. See Reed 36. In an interview on December 7, 1999, Lucas told me that she also remembers the sisters telling people that they were cousins to Walt Whitman and when she was in their home she saw a set of dishes the sisters said belonged to Walt Whitman. Nonetheless, she doubts the veracity of the claim. See also Lucas, 424.

44. For critical analysis of Reverend Whitman's poetry and discussions of other nineteenth-century poets see Joan R. Sherman, *Invisible Poets: Afro-Americans of the Nineteenth Century* (Chicago: University of Illinois Press, 1974), and Joan R. Sherman, *African-American Poetry of the Nineteenth Century.*

45. In *Invisible Poets,* Joan Sherman cites a critic who admired Reverend Whitman's poem *Not a Man and Yet a Man* but decried his enslavement to alcohol. She speculates that alcohol may have hastened his death because "debility" (a euphemism) was listed on his death certificate as the contributory cause.

46. This money may have come from a combination of his salary as a minister and any pay he received for his poetry. His collection of poems *Essays on the Ten Plagues and Miscellaneous Poems* (ca. 1871) is known to have sold about 1,000 copies, though none of these has survived.

47. *The Birmingham News*, February 22, 1902.

48. For a discussion of black women and the Great Migration see Jacqueline Jones, *Labor of Love, Labor of Sorrow: Black Women, Work, and the Family From Slavery to the Present* (New York: Basic Books, 1985).

49. *The Washington Bee*, May 23, 1908.

50. *The Washington Bee*, May 23, 1908.

51. *The Washington Bee*, June 13, 1908.

52. *The Washington Bee*, June 13, 1908.

53. Sources differ on whether or not Alice was a "blood" relation. Lucas claims that Alice was adopted and based on documents pertaining to the death of her son, Albert, speculates that her real last name may have been Harp. Efforts to locate adoption papers (if they exist) have been fruitless. Lucas claims that soon after her husband's death, Caddie Whitman found the young unkempt Alice playing alone on the railroad tracks and upon bringing her home, her mother told Caddie to keep her because she didn't want her. Alice, as an adult, apparently visited her mother and decided to stay a Whitman. Lucas speculates that Alice may have been considerably lighter than her birth mother, prompting scandal about her biological father. From all accounts however, Alice was certainly considered an important member of the central company (the four sisters). If the circumstances of her "adoption" are true, they foreshadow a practice that was to occur many times with the company—several talented children were "adopted" by the Whitman sisters. I discuss this in further detail in the next chapter. See Lucas, 427.

54. Bernard L. Peterson, *The African American Theatre Directory, 1816-1960: A Comprehensive Guide to Early Black Theatre Organizations, Companies, Theatres, and Performing Groups* (Westport, CT: Greenwood Press, 1997), 202.

55. *The Washington Bee*, October 24, 1914.

56. *The Chicago Defender*, January 26, 1918.

57. Interview with Buster Brown by Dianne Walker, Oral History Project, Dance Collection, New York Public Library, Saturday, February 8, 1997, 5 P.M.

58. By bodily memories, I refer to dances and rituals that were transmitted and remembered in the body, through movement and gesture rather than by writing down directions.

59. Mr. Brown's first name has been alternately given as William and Henry. Some scholars speculate that this was William Wells Brown, but the birth and death dates appear to disprove this claim.

60. Orlando Patterson, "Rethinking Black History," *African Report* 17.9 (1972): 29-31.

61. George Pullen Jackson, *White and Negro Spirituals, Their Life Span and Kinship* (Locust Valley, NY: J. J. Augustin, 1943), 293.

62. For a detailed discussion on African influences in American culture see Brenda Dixon-Gottschild, *Digging the Africanist Presence in American Performance: Dance and Other Contexts* (Westport, CT: Greenwood Press, 1996). See also the articles in section 1 of Errol Hill, *The Theatre of Black Americans: A Collection of Critical Essays* (New York: Applause Theatre Book Publishers, 1987). Jacqui Malone begins her book *Steppin' on the Blues: The Visible Rhythms of African American Dance* (Chicago: University of Illinois Press, 1996) with a discussion of the Africanisms that have influenced African American dance.

63. Eileen Southern, "An Origin for the Negro Spiritual," *The Theatre of Black Americans: A Collection of Critical Essays*, ed. Errol Hill (New York: Applause Theatre Book Publishers, 1987): 80-98.

64. For an in-depth discussion of memory, see James V. Hatch, "Here Comes Everybody: Scholarship and Black Theater History." In *Interpreting the Theatrical Past*, ed. Thomas Postlewait and Bruce A. McConachie (Iowa City: University of Iowa Press, 1989).

65. See Toni Morrison, "The Site of Memory," in *Out There: Marginalization and Contemporary Cultures*, ed. Russell Ferguson et al. (Cambridge: MIT Press, 1990).

66. See Eleanor Traylor, "Two Afro-American Contributions to Dramatic Form." In *The Theatre of Black Americans: A Collection of Critical Essays*, ed. Errol Hill (New York: Applause Theatre Book Publishers, 1987), 45-60. Also, for an example of work done to record the invaluable knowledge transmitted by African American elders, see the work of Beverly Robinson, especially *Aunt (Ant Phyllis)*, (Berkeley, CA: Regent Press, 1989).

67. Two of the most recent books on African American dance history do an excellent job tracing the Africanist presence in American cultural production. See Malone, *Steppin' On the Blues: The Visible Rhythms of African American Dance*, and Gottschild, *Digging the Africanist Presence in American Performance.* See also Stearns, *Jazz Dance*, 14-15. In this text, the Stearnses have identified six characteristics of African dance that are helpful in tracing this history:

    1. It is danced on the naked earth with bare feet, often flat-footed glides, drags, or shuffles.
    2. It is usually performed in a crouched position.
    3. Animals are often imitated in realistic detail.
    4. There is great emphasis placed on improvisation, often satirical, that allows for freedom of expression.

5. It is centrifugal, exploding outward from the hips.

6. It is performed to a propulsive rhythm.

68. Stearns, 88. The Stearnses describe the African and African American roots of Georgia Hunchin' (or "truckin,'" as it was also known) on pages 13, 30, and 233.

69. For further discussion of the social significance of the Cakewalk, see Gottschild 114ff.

70. Geneviève Fabre, "African-American Commemorative Celebrations in the Nineteenth Century." In *History & Memory in African-American Culture*, ed. Geneviève Fabre and Robert O'Meally (Oxford UP, 1994), 72.

71. Robert Hinton, "Black Dance in American History," *American Dance Festival: The Black Tradition in American Modern Dance* (Durham, NC: American Dance Festival, 1988), 4.

72. Lynn Fauley Emery, *Black Dance: From 1619 to Today* (Princeton, NJ: Princeton Book Company, 1988), 61-62. See also Leni Sloan's interview in *Ethnic Notions*, Marlon Riggs, dir. (San Francisco, CA: California Newsreel, 1986).

73. Federal Writers' Project, *Slave Narratives*, XVI, Part 4, p. 198.

74. *Statutes at Large of South Carolina*, Vol. VII. Act of 1740. No. 670 Sec. XXXVI.

75. Emery, 121.

76. Stearns, 99.

77. Emery, 93-94.

78. Bennie Butler, "The Whitman Sisters and Moten's Band at Lafayette," *The Inter-State Tattler*, December 17, 1931.

79. Stearns, 14-15.

80. Stearns, 88.

81. Malone, 33.

82. In the next chapter, I comment on these and other repertory choices, particularly interrogating the politics of cross-dressing and image.

83. Langston Hughes and Milton Meltzer, *Black Magic*, 48.

84. Hughes and Meltzer, 48.

85. For a detailed discussion of this theater company see Marvin Edward McAllister, *"White People Do Not Know How to Behave at Entertainments Designed For Ladies and Gentlemen of Color": A History of New York's African Grove/African Theatre*, Ph.D. diss., Theatre and Drama, Northwestern University, 1997.

86. In the next chapter, I analyze the ways in which the Whitman Sisters handled these tensions.

87. Robert C. Toll, *Blacking Up: The Minstrel Show in Nineteenth Century America* (New York: Oxford UP, 1974), 28.

88. Gottschild explores the claims of "authenticity" by locating Africanist products expropriated in minstrelsy in *Digging the Africanist Presence in American Performance: Dance and Other Contexts*.

89. Toll, 38. See also Eric Lott, *Love and Theft: Blackface Minstrelsy and the American Working Class* (New York: Oxford UP, 1995), 20.

90. Toll, 33.

91. Marlon Riggs, *Ethnic Notions*, video recording (San Francisco: California Newsreel, 1986).

92. Gottschild, 84.

93. Riggs.

94. In the next chapter I analyze the ways in which the Whitman Sisters dealt with the legacy of minstrelsy especially in terms of the image of Mammy.

95. For further discussion on the complexities of influence in minstrelsy, see Lott, *Love and Theft*, and Howard L. Sacks and Judith Rose Sacks, *Way Up North in Dixie: A Black Family's Claim to the Confederate Anthem* (Washington, D.C.: Smithsonian Institution Press, 1996).

96. See Stearns, 189, and Rusty E. Frank, *Tap! The Greatest Tap Dance Stars and Their Stories, 1900-1955* (New York: Da Capo Press, 1994), 21.

97. The Nicholas brothers vehemently denied this claim, although, as Edward Thorpe observed, they certainly saw Robinson and Alice Whitman at the Standard Theatre in Philadelphia when they were just starting out. See Edward Thorpe, *Black Dance* (Woodstock, NY: Overlook Press, 1990), 102.

98. Stearns, 88.

99. Bennie Butler.

100. For an interesting collection of materials on these genres, see the Library of Congress, Rare Books and Special Collections, American Variety Stage.

101. The Whitman Sisters had a complex negotiation around the politics of respectability, which I discuss in detail in the next chapter.

102. Black vaudeville led to the extremely successful decades of black musical theater of the Harlem Renaissance and beyond. Some performers like the Whitman Sisters were able to thrive even as the tide was turning away from vaudeville. I discuss the later history of black vaudeville and the Whitman Sisters in the last section of this book.

103. Helen Armstead-Johnson, "Themes and Values in Afro-American Librettos and Book Musicals, 1898-1930." In *Musical Theatre in America: Papers and Proceedings of the Conference on the Musical in Theatre in America*, ed. Glenn Loney (Westport, CT: Greenwood Press, 1984), 134.

104. *The Washington Bee*, May 9, 1908.

105. For programs of other black vaudeville performances, see Sampson, *The Ghost Walks*.

106. I use interviews from various newspaper articles, interviews by the Stearnses, and secondary sources.

107. Stearns, 89.

108. *The Washington Bee,* May 23, 1908.

109. For reviews of the Whitman Sisters see: *The Birmingham News,* February 22, 1902; *The Springfield News,* October 8, 1906; *The Courier Citizen,* January 1, 1907; *The Washington Bee,* May 9, 1908; *The Washington Bee,* May 23, 1908; *The Washington Bee,* June 13, 1908; *The Morning Times,* December 26, 1908; *The Indianapolis Freeman,* December 25, 1915; *The Chicago Defender,* January 26, 1918.

110. Hay, 170.

111. Stearns, 91.

112. Frank, 122.

113. Stearns, 91.

114. Sampson, 321.

115. Bennie Moten's band would go on to popularize big-band jazz at the Savoy in the 1930s. See Stearns, 325.

116. *The Washington Bee,* May 30, 1908. An example of the type of information that Mabel might divulge in these addresses can be found in an interview with her conducted by *The Chicago Defender,* which appeared January 26, 1918.

117. Thomas L. Riis, *Just Before Jazz: Black Musical Theater in New York, 1890 to 1915* (Washington, D.C.: Smithsonian Institution Press, 1989), 88.

118. *The Courier-Citizen,* January 1, 1907.

119. *The Courier-Citizen,* January 1, 1907.

120. Bennie Butler, "The Whitman Sisters and Moten's Band at Lafayette," *The Inter-State Tattler,* December 17, 1931.

121. *The Courier-Citizen,* January 1, 1907.

122. *The Springfield News,* October 8, 1906.

123. *The Indianapolis Freeman,* December 25, 1915.

124. Stearns, 91.

125. Stearns, 90.

126. Frank, 122.

127. According to Ernestine Lucas there was a Princess Wee Wee who was also part of the Ringling Bros. and Barnum & Bailey Circus. This may or may not have been the same Princess Wee Wee who appeared with the Whitmans Sisters. It is possible that she made appearances for both organizations.

128. Reed, 42.

129. Stearns, 89.

130. Lucas, 339.

131. Stearns, 87.

132. Stearns, 80.

133. Riis, 51-52.
134. A late-twentieth-century example might be the relationship between Al and Peg Bundy in the television sitcom "Married with Children" if the sexual innuendo were omitted.
135. For a script of one of their acts see Leo Hamalian and James V. Hatch, *The Roots of African American Drama: An Anthology of Early Plays, 1858-1938* (Detroit: Wayne State UP, 1991), 155-158.
136. Stearns, 88-89.
137. Interview with Buster Brown by Dianne Walker.
138. Frank, 122.
139. Stearns, 88.
140. Stearns, 86.
141. *The Indianapolis Freeman*, December 25, 1915.
142. Stearns, 90.
143. Stearns, 91.
144. Stearns, 91.

CHAPTER 3: RACE, GENDER, AND CLASS

1. According to Ernestine Lucas, the sisters' great grandfather was the child of a white woman in Kentucky. Personal interview, December 7, 1999.
2. Class as an identity category is intricately interrelated to race and gender for the Whitman sisters. In fact, much of the reason they were able to effect so many transgressions in terms of race and gender was because of the ways in which they cultivated class. However, because class operates differently as a socially constructed category, I discuss class in detail in the next section.
3. Judith Butler, *Bodies That Matter: On the Discursive Limits of Sex* (New York: Routledge, 1993), 95. For further discussion of gender identity as a performative act compelled by social sanction and taboo see Butler's article "Performative Acts and Gender Constitution: An Essay in Phenomenology and Feminist Theory," in *Performing Feminisms: Feminist Critical Theory and Theatre*, ed. Sue-Ellen Case (Baltimore: Johns Hopkins UP, 1990).
4. Butler, 95.
5. Although inadequate for analyzing the complexities of identity, I use the term *binaries* here to describe the historical categorizations at work during the turn of the century.
6. For a detailed examination of semiotics in feminist performance theory see Sue-Ellen Case, *Feminism and Theatre* (New York: Routledge, 1988), 115ff.
7. *Ethnic Notions* (video recording). San Francisco: California Newsreel, 1986.
8. Chris Shilling, *The Body and Social Theory* (London: Sage Publications, 1993), 3.

9.   For a detailed discussion of identity as construction of race, gender, and class see Evelyn Brooks Higginbotham, "African-American Women's History and the Metalanguage of Race," in *We Specialize in the Wholly Impossible: A Reader in Black Women's History*, ed. Darlene Clark Hine, et al. (New York: Carlson, 1995), 487-503.

10. Shilling, 74.

11. Michael Omi and Howard Winant, *Racial Formation in the United States: From 1960s to the 1990s* (New York: Routledge, 1994), 68.

12. For an introduction to Foucault's theories on the body, one may begin with Michel Foucault, *The History of Sexuality: An Introduction*, Vols. 1, 2, and 3 (New York: Vintage Books, 1978), and Michel Foucault, *Discipline and Punish: The Birth of The Prison* (New York: Vintage Books, 1979).

13. Michel Foucault, *The History of Sexuality: An Introduction*, Vol. 1 (New York: Vintage Books, 1978), 139.

14. Michel Foucault, *Discipline and Punish* 200.

15. Jill Dolan, *The Feminist Spectator as Critic* (Ann Arbor: University of Michigan Press), 116.

16. Gillian Rose, *Feminism and Geography: The Limits of Geographical Knowledge* (Minneapolis: University of Minnesota Press, 1993), 32.

17. For examples of theater scholars applying feminist film theory to theater, see Gayle Austin, *Feminist Theories for Dramatic Criticism* (Ann Arbor: University of Michigan Press, 1990), and Elaine Aston, *An Introduction to Feminism and Theatre* (New York: Routledge, 1995).

18. Laura Mulvey, "Visual Pleasure and Narrative Cinema," in *Art After Modernism: Rethinking Representation*, ed. Brian Wallis (New York: The New Museum of Contemporary Art, 1984), 366.

19. Mulvey, 366.

20. Elaine Aston, *An Introduction to Feminism and Theatre* (New York: Routledge, 1995), 43. For more on the female gaze see also Jill Dolan, *The Feminist Spectator as Critic*.

21. Mulvey, 373.

22. Multiple spectatorship is hardly unique to the Whitman Sisters. Many theatrical experiences can be examined from the points of view of different audience members based on race, class, gender, sexual orientation, and so on. For other examples of this type of investigation see Bruce A. McConachie, "Using the Concept of Cultural Hegemony to Write Theatre History," and Marvin Carlson "Theatre Audiences and the Reading of Performance," both in *Interpreting the Theatrical Past: Essays in the Historiography of Performance*, ed. Thomas Postlewait and Bruce A. McConachie (Iowa City: University of Iowa Press, 1991).

23. I discuss the complexities of class in the next section, but for our purposes here, it is enough to argue that based primarily on economics, perhaps always the driving factor, the Whitman Sisters valued high-class spectators, yet remained a valuable part of more popular culture. Although focused on attracting the members of society able to pay higher prices, they nonetheless maintained appeal to a larger segment of the population. This was the goal for many vaudeville performers. No company intentionally built its reputation as low-class entertainment. This would have been theatrical suicide. Although forms such as burlesque and variety were often considered lower forms of popular entertainment, most performers strove to make it to the big time and play legitimate theaters.

24. Gottschild, *Digging the Africanist Presence in American Performance: Dance and Other Contexts* (Westport, CT: Greenwood Press, 1996), 85.

25. See Henry Louis Gates, *The Signifying Monkey: A Theory of African American Literary Criticism* (New York: Oxford UP, 1988).

26. For detailed definitions see Gates, 52ff.

27. Sandra L. Richards, "Writing the Absent Potential: Drama, Performance, and the Canon of African American Literature," in *Performativity and Performance*, ed. Andrew Parker and Eve Kosofsky Sedgwick (New York: Routledge, 1995), 65.

28. Butler, 123.

29. Gates, 124.

30. Quoted in Rudi Blesh and Harriet Janis, *They All Played Ragtime* (New York: Alfred A. Knopf, 1950), 96.

31. Interestingly, we may also read Mammy's big bright smile as part of the tradition of trickstering in which she used guile and seeming compliance in dealing with the master in order to get what she wanted. While seemingly complicit, Mammy often found a way to improve her life. For an example see Langston Hughes' Cora in *The Mulatto*, in *Five Plays by Langston Hughes*, ed. Webster Smalley (Bloomington: Indiana UP, 1963), 1-38.

32. See K. Sue Jewell, *From Mammy to Miss America and Beyond: Cultural Images and the Shaping of U.S. Policy* (New York: Routledge, 1993), 36, 42, and Marlon Riggs, producer, writer, director, *Ethnic Notions* (video recording). San Francisco: California Newsreel, 1986.

33. Riggs.

34. For radical re-visioning of the image of Mammy see Breena Clark and Glenda Dickerson, "Re/membering Aunt Jemima: Rescuing the Secret Voice," *Women and Performance* 6.1 (1993). For a discussion of the image of Mammy as part of the market economy see Kenneth W. Goings, *Mammy and Uncle Mose: Black Collectibles and American Stereotyping* (Bloomington: Indiana UP, 1994). For a discussion of the social impact of the image of Mammy see K. Sue Jewell, *From*

Mammy to Miss America and Beyond, and Marlon, Riggs, *Ethnic Notions*. For a feminist analysis of Mammy see Patricia Hill Collins, *Black Feminist Thought: Knowledge, Consciousness, and the Politics of Empowerment* (New York: Routledge, 1991).

35. *Minstrel-Show Songs* (New York: Da Capo Press, 1980), 20.

36. James Weldon Johnson, *The Book of American Negro Spirituals* (New York: Viking Press, 1925), 30-33.

37. To compare minstrel songs with jubilee songs in terms of the representation of African American life one might look at James Weldon Johnson, *The Book of American Negro Spirituals;* J. B. T. Marsh, *The Story of the Jubilee Singers; with Their Songs* (New York: Negro Universities Press, 1969); and *Minstrel-Show Songs*.

38. For a discussion of how this practice worked in dramas between 1890 and 1920 see Judith L. Stephens, "Gender Ideology and Dramatic Convention in Progressive Era Plays, 1890-1920," *Performing Feminisms: Feminist Critical Theory and Theatre*, ed. Sue-Ellen Case (Baltimore: Johns Hopkins UP, 1990), 283ff.

39. Dickerson, 111. Dickerson succeeds in reclaiming these images in her play with Breena Clark, "Re/membering Aunt Jemima: A Menstrual Show," reprinted in *Colored Contradictions: An Anthology of Contemporary African-American Plays*, ed. Harry J. Elam and Robert Alexander (New York: Plume, 1996), 141-171.

40. Alice Walker, "Giving the Party: Aunt Jemima, Mammy and the Goddess Within," *Ms.* 4.6 (1994): 22.

41. Walker, "Giving the Party," 23.

42. Sampson, *The Ghost Walks*, 284, and Anthony Slide, *The Encyclopedia of Vaudeville* (Westport, CT: Greenwood Press, 1994), 50.

43. Sampson, *The Ghost Walks*, 284.

44. Thorpe, *Black Dance* (Woodstock, NY: Overlook Press), 108.

45. Slide, *The Encyclopedia of Vaudeville*, 50.

46. Stearns, *Jazz Dance: The Story of American Vernacular Dance* (New York: Da Capo Press, 1994), 86.

47. Elaine Ginsberg, *Passing and the Fictions of Identity* (Durham, NC: Duke UP, 1996), 4.

48. Jo A. Tanner, *Dusky Maidens: The Odyssey of the Early Black Dramatic Actress* (Westport, CT: Greenwood Press, 1992), 109.

49. Nella Larsen, *Quicksand and Passing* (New Brunswick, NJ: Rutgers UP, 1986), 185-186.

50. Rusty E. Frank, *Tap! The Greatest Tap Dance Stars and Their Stories, 1900-1955* (New York: Da Capo Press, 1994),45.

51. Stearns, 86.

52. *Jet*, January 30, 1969.

53. Ginsberg, 7.

54. bell hooks, *Black Looks: Race and Representation* (Boston, MA: South End Press, 1992), 115.

55. Sampson, *The Ghost Walks*, 198.

56. In a telephone interview on December 10, 1999, Ernestine Lucas pointed out that since slave performance comprised of mostly dark-skinned field hands being asked up to the big house, lighter black people in show business was unusual and some upper class light-skinned African Americans did not approve. However, according to Lucas, the Whitman sisters "felt so black" that it did not matter that they were not dark. Their hearts were with the black community.

57. Trezzvant W. Anderson, "Whitman Sisters Rounding Out 20th Year on Stage as One Unit," *Baltimore Afro-American*, December 1931. It is interesting that the newspaper editor found it necessary to qualify Mabel's statement with the word "humorously" lest the reader misinterpret her.

58. Tony Langston, "Whitman Sisters Open Good Show at the Grand," *Chicago Defender*, June 21, 1924.

59. Allen Woll, *Black Musical Theatre: From Coontown to Dreamgirls* (New York: Da Capo Press, 1989), 113.

60. Tanner, 132.

61. Frank, 122.

62. E-mail interview with Deborah Kirtman, April 29, 1999.

63. Audre Lorde, *Sister Outsider: Essays and Speeches* (Freedom, CA: The Crossing Press, 1984), 53-59.

64. Interview with Leonard Reed by Fred Stickler, Oral History Project, Dance Collection, New York Public Library.

65. Tony Langston, "Whitman Sisters Open Good Show at the Grand," *Chicago Defender*, June 21, 1924.

66. Frank, 126-127.

67. Frank, 126.

68. Interview for New York Public Library.

69. Stearns, 88.

70. Col. Brown and Staff, "The Lincoln," *Indianapolis Freeman*, December 25, 1915.

71. Stearns, 88.

72. For more on the breeches role see Tracy C. Davis, *Actresses as Working Women: Their Social Identity in Victorian Culture* (New York: Routledge, 1991), 108-116, and Laurence Senelick, "Boys and Girls Together: Subcultural Origins of Glamour Drag and Male Impersonation on the Nineteenth-Century Stage," *Crossing the Stage: Controversies on Cross-Dressing*, ed. Lesley Farris (New York: Routledge, 1993), 81. For more on the travesty dancer and nineteenth century

gender politics see Lynn Garafola, "The Travesty Dancer in Nineteenth-Century Ballet," *Crossing the Stage*, 96-106.

73.   Senelick, 81.

74.   Although it is beyond the scope of this book to delve too deeply into a discussion of the sisters' sexuality, according to Leonard Reed, Alberta did not think of herself as a man. Though noteworthy, this one comment is hardly enough to draw conclusions with any certainty. There is no extant evidence to support further claims. Other female performers cross-dressed; most notably, black dancer Florence Hines also performed as a male impersonator. See Sampson, *The Ghost Walks*, 183.

75.   For a good introduction to theories on cross-dressing in theater see the articles in *Crossing the Stage*. For an interesting discussion on dress as an indication and producer of gender see Ruth Barnes and Joanne B. Eicher, ed., *Dress and Gender: Making and Meaning* (Oxford: Berg, 1992).

76.   Interestingly, Europe was even less accommodating of cross-dressing in public than the United States as most European cities had laws prohibiting public cross-dressing. Transvestite women in Berlin and St. Petersburg were regularly arrested. For more on the ways in which women cross-dressed in public in the United States see Senelick, "Boys and Girls Together: Subcultural Origins of Glamour Drag and Male Impersonation on the Nineteenth-Century Stage," 89.

77.   Senelick claims that the popularity of cross-dressing that began in the 1860s was an outgrowth of a newly conspicuous homosexual subculture, which provided wish fulfillment for the rest of society. Although Alberta was certainly building on this popularity, I hesitate to make similar claims until more work is done in drag and queer theory that historicizes and incorporates racial politics.

78.   Senelick, 93.

79.   Butler, 125.

80.   Dolan, 116.

81.   *The Washington Bee*, May 30, 1908.

82.   Bennie Butler, "The Whitman Sisters and Moten's Band at Lafayette," *The Inter-State Tattler*, December 17, 1931. My emphasis.

83.   For the Whitmans there were, of course, the added difficulties of maintaining a public life and running and performing in a popular theater company.

84.   For a discussion of the image of African American women throughout history, see K. Sue Jewell, *From Mammy to Miss America and Beyond*.

85.   Evelyn Brooks Higginbotham, *Righteous Discontent: The Women's Movement in the Black Baptist Church, 1880-1920* (Cambridge, MA: Harvard UP, 1993), 202.

86.   For a discussion of the politics of black women adopting Victorian ideology, see Darlene Clark Hine, "Rape and the Inner Lives of Black Women in the

Middle West: Preliminary Thoughts on the Culture of Dissemblance," *Signs* 14.4 (Summer 1989): 915. Also, Glenda Dickerson provides a contemporary analysis of this "cult" and black women in "The Cult of True Womanhood: Toward a Womanist Attitude in African-American Theatre," in *Performing Feminisms: Feminist Critical Theory and Theatre*.

87. For a discussion of the tenets of the Cult of True Womanhood, see Barbara Welter's *Dimity Convictions: The American Woman in the Nineteenth Century* (Athens: Ohio UP, 1976), 21-41. And for a discussion on Victorian gender ideology including sentimentalism, Christianity, charity, courtship and domesticity, see Gail Parker's *The Oven Birds: American Woman on Womanhood, 1820-1920* (Garden City, NY: Anchor Books, 1972).

88. Higginbotham, *Righteous Discontent*, 192.

89. Higginbotham, *Righteous Discontent*, 187.

90. Higginbotham, *Righteous Discontent*, 204.

91. Stephens, 284, 286-7.

92. Higginbotham, *Righteous Discontent*, 1.

93. Higginbotham, *Righteous Discontent*, 14.

94. Reed, 38.

95. "Whitman Sisters' Tent Theatre at Forty-Sixth Street and Wabash Avenue," *Pittsburgh Courier*, August 20, 1927.

96. Muse, 66.

97. In his interview for the New York Public Library, Leonard Reed admits to having lied about being an orphan.

98. Trezzvant W. Anderson, "Whitman Sisters Rounding out 20th Year on Stage as One Unit," *Baltimore Afro-American*, December 1931.

99. Muse, 67.

100. Interview with Buster Brown by Dianne Walker, Oral History Project, Dance Collection, New York Public Library. Saturday, February 8, 1997, 5:00 P.M.

101. For more work on the politics of the racial uplift movement see also: Lindsay Elizabeth Davis, *Lifting as They Climb* (Washington, D.C.: National Association of Colored J. W. Women, n.d.); Anna Julia Cooper, *A Voice From the South* (New York: Oxford UP, 1988); and Alfred A. Moss, *The American Negro Academy: Voice of the Talented Tenth* (Baton Rouge: Louisiana State UP, 1981). For a look at how writers incorporated this ideology see Effie T. Battle, Gertrude Arquene Fisher, and Myra Viola Wilds, *Six Poets of Racial Uplift (African-American Women Writers, 1910-1940)* (New York: GK Hall, 1996), and Hazel V. Carby, *Reconstructing Womanhood: The Emergence of the Afro-American Woman Novelist* (New York: Oxford UP, 1987), 90-94.

102. For a discussion of black women and racial uplift see Linda Perkins, "Black Women and the Philosophy of 'Race Uplift' Prior to Emancipation" (Cam-

bridge, MA: Mary Ingraham Bunting Institute, Radcliffe College, 1980), and "Black Feminism and 'Race Uplift,' 1890-1900" (Institute for Independent Study, Radcliffe College, 1981).

103. Kevin K. Gaines, *Uplifting the Race: Black Leadership, Politics, and Culture in the Twentieth Century* (Chapel Hill: University of North Carolina Press, 1996), 4.

104. For further discussion on racial uplift and the national club movement, see Gerda Lerner, *Black Women in America: A Documentary History* (New York: Pantheon Books, 1972), 437ff, and Gerda Lerner, *The Majority Finds Its Past: Placing Women in History* (New York: Oxford UP, 1979), 74, 85ff.

105. W. E. B. Du Bois, *The Souls of Black Folk* (New York: Penguin Group, 1969).

106. Gaines, xv.

107. Welter, 21-41.

108. We know that Mabel was married to the performers' tutor Dave Payton, Alberta to performer Maxie McCree, and Alice to performer Aaron Palmer. In 1963, Alice remarried, to Len McCowan in Chicago. Alberta also remarried, to a man named Abdeen Ali and later to Virgil Bright, with whom she lived in Arizona long after the company disbanded. Early records show Essie's married name to be Ishmael, though a first name for her husband has not surfaced in any documentation.

109. For a discussion of women in the uplift movement, education, employment, and social service work and a discussion of the tensions and interactions between forms of race and gender discrimination and black women's responses to them, see Cynthia Neverdon-Morton, *Afro-American Women of the South and the Advancement of the Race, 1895-1925* (Knoxville: University of Tennessee Press, 1989).

110. Paula Giddings, *When and Where I Enter: The Impact of Black Women on Race and Sex in America* (New York: Bantam Books, 1984), 113.

111. Louis H. Harlon, ed., *The Booker T. Washington Papers,* Vol. 3 (Chicago: University of Illinois Press, 1974), 444.

112. For a discussion of the impact of these choices on black women's lives, especially Mary Church Terrell, Ida Wells-Barnett, and Margaret Murray Washington, see Giddings 108-112.

113. See Jacqueline Jones, *Labor of Love, Labor of Sorrow: Black Women, Work, and the Family From Slavery to the Present* (New York: Basic Books, 1985), for an interesting discussion of the ways in which these schools were designed in part to professionalize what black women had been doing under slavery and to provide more effective competition against European immigrants who were making inroads as domestic servants in the North.

114. *The Washington Bee,* May 23, 1908.

115. Robert W. Snyder, *The Voice of the City: Vaudeville and Popular Culture in New York* (New York: Oxford UP, 1989), 30.

116. Ethel Waters, *His Eye is on the Sparrow* (New York: Jove Publications, 1982), 93.

117. "Hear What the Press Has to Say," *The Washington Bee*, May 23, 1908.

118. Higginbotham, *Righteous Discontent*, 223.

119. Gaines, 76.

120. For a discussion on the "immorality" of popular entertainment see Daphne Duval Harrison, *Black Pearls: Blues Queens of the 1920s* (New Brunswick, NJ: Rutgers UP, 1993), 30-41.

121. Ernestine Lucas claims that there was no minstrelsy in the Whitman Sister's act. However, from newspaper descriptions of performances it is clear that some elements remained though the derogatory connotations were removed or greatly reduced. See Lucas, *Wider Windows to the Past: African American History from a Family Perspective* (Decorah, IA: Anundsen, 1995), 423.

122. Lucas, 423-24.

123. Gaines, 78

124. The sisters' light skin color no doubt helped in this endeavor.

125. David Krasner, *Resistance, Parody, and Double Consciousness in African American Theatre, 1895-1910* (New York: St. Martin's Press, 1997), 39.

126. "The Whitmans," *The Chicago Defender*, January 26, 1918.

127. Trezzvant W. Anderson, "Whitman Sisters Rounding out 20th Year on Stage as One Unit," *Baltimore Afro-American*, December 1931.

128. Anderson, "Whitman Sisters Rounding out 20th Year."

129. Some of the white vaudeville houses the Whitman Sisters played include the Pantages, the Keith & Proctor circuit, all of the Percy C. Williams houses, the Poli and Fox circuits, the Hammerstein theaters, and many of the leading white houses in New York. In the later years however, they played mainly to black houses, and during the 1920s joined the black touring circuit Toby. See Stearns, 79.

130. *The Washington Bee*, May 23, 1908.

131. "Mae Whitman, 'Boss' of the Famed Musical Hit, is Show Game's Most Original Woman" *Pittsburgh Courier*, March, 13, 1930.

132. *Baltimore Afro-American*, December 1931.

133. Reed, 33.

134. "Mabel of Whitman Sisters Has a Word to Say; Listen," *Chicago Defender*, September 29, 1934.

135. *Pittsburgh Courier*, March 13, 1930.

136. *Pittsburgh Courier*, March 13, 1930.

137. *Pittsburgh Courier*, March 13, 1930.

138. Riis, 18.

139. Sampson, 230. The White Rats were very vocal in their opposition to black and white performers' sharing a stage. For the most part, they were successful although, as mentioned earlier, some black acts did play on white circuits.

140. Sampson, *The Ghost Walks*, 70-71.
141. Willa E. Daughtry, *Sissieretta Jones: A Study of the Negro's Contribution to the Nineteenth-Century American Concert and Theatrical Life*, Diss., Syracuse U., 1968 (Ann Arbor: University of Michigan Press, 1968 [68-13,823]), 91, and Sampson, *The Ghost Walks*, 103.
142. For further discussion on the reluctance of black mothers to send their children into show business, see David Krasner's work on Ada Walker, performance, and racial uplift in *Resistance, Parody, and Double Consciousness in African American Theatre*, 83-84.
143. "Pioneers Pay Price," *Pittsburgh Courier*, September 24, 1924. Reprinted in *Chicago Defender*, September 27, 1924.
144. Stearns, 90.
145. Stearns, 86.
146. Interview for New York Public Library.
147. For a discussion of the different kinship categories of the social system approach to studying families, including nuclear, extended, and augmented families, see Andrew Billingsley's *Black Families in White America* (Englewood Cliffs, NJ: Prentice Hall, 1968), 16ff.
148. Elmer P. Martin and Joanne Mitchell Martin, *The Black Extended Family* (Chicago: University of Chicago Press, 1978), 39.
149. For case studies on the extended black family see Demitri B. Shimkin et al., *The Extended Family in Black Societies* (Chicago: Aldine, 1978).
150. Gerda Lerner, *The Majority Finds Its Past: Placing Women in History* (New York: Oxford UP, 1979), 74.
151. Sampson, *The Ghost Walks*, 321.
152. Sampson, *The Ghost Walks*, 321.
153. Woll, 52.
154. Riis, 160.
155. *Baltimore Afro-American*, January 19, 1929.
156. Stearns, 87.
157. Samuel Hay, *African American Theatre: A Historical and Critical Analysis* (New York: Cambridge UP, 1994), 170.
158. James Weldon Johnson, *Black Manhattan* (New York: A. A. Knopf, 1930), 170.
159. Woll, 50.

CHAPTER 4: TOBY, THE DEPRESSION, AND BEYOND

1. *The 1928 Official Theatrical World of Colored Artists*, pamphlet.
2. Langston Hughes and Milton Meltzer, *Black Magic: A Pictorial History of the African American in the Performing Arts* (New York: Da Capo Press, 1990), 67.

3. Charles Samuels and Louise Samuels, *Once Upon a Stage: The Merry World of Vaudeville* (New York: Dodd, Mead and Company, 1974), 264. Bill Smith, *The Vaudevillians* (New York: Macmillan, 1976), 16,

4. Thomas L. Riis, *Just Before Jazz: Black Musical Theatre in New York, 1890 to 1915* (Washington, D.C.: Smithsonian Institution Press, 1994), 18.

5. For more on the early performing career of S. H. Dudley see Riis, 141, and New York Public Library Billy Rose special collections at Lincoln Center.

6. *The 1928 Official Theatrical World of Colored Artists* has an ad for TOBA listing C. H. Turpin as president (Booker Washington Theatre, St. Louis, MO), Sam E. Reevin as treasurer and manager (Volunteer Building, Chattanooga, TN), Martin Klein as manager of the western office (Overton building, 3621 South State Street, Chicago, IL) and S. H. Dudley as manager of the eastern office (1223 Seventh Street N. W., Washington, D.C.).

7. For a discussion of Toby's importance in the music industry, see Daphne Duval Harrison, *black Pearls: Blues Queens of the 1920s* (New Brunswick, NJ: Rutgers University Press, 1993), 17.

8. *The Roots Of "One Mo' Time,"* Solters & Roskin, INC. Public Relations Materials, press release.

9. For further discussion of the ill treatment of performers by whites see Daphne Duval Harrison, 25-41.

10. Sampson, 198.

11. Interview with Leonard Reed.

12. Daphne Harrison, 27-28; "S. H. Dudley: Veteran Producer and Vice-President and Eastern Representative of The Theater Owners' Booking Association," *The Messenger* (January 1925): 50-52.

13. *Chicago Defender*, December 5, 1925, 6.

14. *Pittsburgh Courier*, November 27, 1926, 8.

15. Stearns, *Jazz Dance: The Story of American Vernacular Dance* (New York: Da Capo Press, 1994), 80.

16. *The Roots of "One Mo' Time."* The history of the Lyric Theater as told to Vernel Bagneris by his grandmother inspired the musical hit *One Mo' Time* (1979).

17. Stearns, 79.

18. Tony Langston, "Whitman Open Good Show at the Grand," *Chicago Defender*, June 21, 1924.

19. Tony Langston, "Whitman Sisters Change at Grand," *Chicago Defender*, June 28, 1924.

20. "Whitmans Meet Coolidge," *Chicago Defender*, July 3, 1926

21. *Chicago Defender*, 27 September 27, 1924.

22. For a discussion of the rise and decline of mainstream American touring companies and legitimate theater, see Jack Poggi's *Theater in America: The Impact*

of Economic Forces 1870-1967 (Ithaca, NY: Cornell UP, 1968).

23. Woll, *Black Musical Theatre: From Coontown to Dreamgirls* (New York: Da Capo Press, 1989), 136.

24. Stearns, 80.

25. Stearns, 140.

26. See the *Chicago Defender*, April 4, 1936.

27. In his interview for the New York Public Library, Leonard Reed claims that after Mabel's death there was nobody left who was skilled enough to handle the company's business affairs. He said, "May died then they died out."

28. Henry T. Sampson, *Blacks in Blackface: A Source Book On Early Black Musical Shows* (Metuchen, NJ: Scarecrow Press, 1980).

29. "Mabel of Whitman Sisters Has a Word to Say; Listen," *Chicago Defender*, September 29, 1934.

30. Reed, 44.

31. Bennie Butler, "The Whitman Sisters and Moten's Band at Lafayette," *The Inter-State Tattler*, Thursday, December 17, 1931.

32. Bennie Butler.

33. Lucas, *Wider Windows to the Past: African American History from a Family Perspective* (Decorah, IA: Anundsen, 1995), 423.

34. The 1928 Official Theatrical World of Colored Artists.

35. Quoted in Lucas, 435.

36. Quoted in Lucas, 441.

37. The *Baltimore Afro-American*, December 17, 1932, gives the show credits as follows:

> Miss Mabel Whitman, owner and producer of this celebrated theatrical troupe is aided by the following personnel for this season: Frank Peyton, business manager; Bert and Alice Whitman, famous song and dance team; Pops Whitman, juvenile tap dancer; and his little partner, Clarence (Groundhog) Taylor; Arnett-Babero, song and dance specialty, and Princess Wee Wee. Troy Snapp, pianist, is director of the orchestra known as the Chicago Night Hawks, which is comprised of Shirrod Smith, saxophonist and vocalist; Clifford Redeaus, saxophone; Lawrence C. Edgeson, trombone; Bob Claybrook, cornet, and J. Leslie Towels, drummer. Joe Hubert is acting as master of ceremonies and also does a number in a style all his own. Buddle Green and John LaRue, well-known comedy team, furnish the laughs. Miss Whitman presents the following girls in a balanced and well-trained chorus; Misses Florence Hayes, Vivian Thompson, Ida Mae Ricks, Jennie LeGon,

Bernice George, Mary E. Brown and Gladys Coleman. Vivian Thompson, likewise, does a very clever toe dancing number. Billie Evans is going over big with her songs, always enthusiastically greeted by the audience.

38. *Baltimore Afro-American Capital Edition,* December 17, 1932.
39. *Chicago Defender,* April 4, 1936.
40. *Chicago Defender,* October 3, 1936.
41. Harry P. Brandon, "Harlem Home of the Stage," *The Philadelphia Tribune,* October 5, 1940.
42. *Baltimore Afro-American,* June 27, 1936.
43. *Chicago Defender,* May 16, 1942.
44. *Chicago Defender,* May 16, 1942.
45. *Daily News,* May 8, 1963.
46. "Terrified By Blaze, Ex Dancer, 81, Dies," *Variety,* May 15, 1963.
47. *Chicago Defender,* June 27, 1964.
48. *Chicago Defender,* June 27, 1964.
49. *Jet,* January 30, 1969.
50. *Jet,* January 30, 1969.
51. Lucas, 441.
52. *Pittsburgh Courier,* September 24, 1924.

Bibliography

ARCHIVES

The Armstead-Johnson Foundation for Theater Research

Beinecke Rare Books Collection at Yale University

The Black Dance Collection in the Multiethnic and Multicultural Christian
    Education and Ministry

Chicago Historical Society

Columbia University—Brander Matheas Dramatic Museum, Rare Book and
    Manuscript Library

Cross-Cultural Dance Resources, Inc., Flagstaff, AZ

Du Bois Institute, Cambridge, MA

DuSable Museum (non display collections)

The E. Azalia Hackley Memorial Collection of Negro Music, Dance, and Drama,
    Detroit, MI

Harvard University Theater Collection

The Hatch-Billops Collection, New York, NY

Howard University Library

The James Weldon Johnson Memorial Collection of Negro Arts and Letters at Yale
    University

The Joe Nash Black Dance Collection

The Library of Congress

Marx Theater Collection at Chicago Public Library

The New York Public Library Lincoln Center for the Performing Arts, Billy Rose
    Collection

Newberry Library, Chicago, IL

Northwestern University Special Collections

Pusey Library, Harvard University

Rutger's Institute for Jazz Study

Schomburg Center for Research in Black Culture

Smithsonian Institute

State Historical Society of Madison, WI

Tuskegee Institute

The Vivian G. Harsh Collection of Afro-American History and Literature

Woodson Regional Library Yale Drama Library

PERIODICALS

Artforum
Baltimore Afro-American
Billboard
Birmingham News
Boston Globe
Chicago Defender
Colored American
Courier-Citizen (Lowell, MA)
Crisis
Daily News
Daily Times (Los Angeles, CA)
Dancemagazine
Dramatic Mirror
Ebony High Performance
Indianapolis Freeman
Inter-State Tattler
Jet
Los Angeles Herald Examiner
Los Angeles Times
Metro and State (Atlanta, GA)
Morning Times (San Jose, CA)
New Dance
New York Age
New York Amsterdam News
New York Times
New York Tribune
News and Courier (Charleston, SC)
Opportunity
Philadelphia Inquirer
Philadelphia Tribune
Pittsburgh Courier
Springfield News (Springfield, MA)
U.S. News and World Report
Variety
Village Voice
Washington Bee

BOOKS

Abramson, Doris E. *Negro Playwrights in the American Theatre, 1925-1959.* New York: Columbia University Press, 1969.

Agger, Ben. *Cultural Studies as Critical Theory.* Washington, DC: Falmer Press, 1992.

Allen, Robert Clyde. *Horrible Prettiness: Burlesque And American Culture.* Chapel Hill: University of North Carolina Press, 1991.

Allen, Zita. "The Great American 'Black Dance' Mystery." *Freedomways* 20.4 (1980): 283-290.

American Dance Festival. The Black Tradition in American Modern Dance. Durham, N.C.: ADF, 1988.

Archer, Leonard Courtney. *Black Images in the American Theatre; NAACP Protest Campaigns—Stage, Screen, Radio & Television.* Brooklyn, N.Y.: Pageant-Poseidon, 1973.

Asante, Molefi Kete. *The Afrocentric Idea.* Philadelphia: Temple University Press, 1987.

———. "Afrocentricity and the Critique of Drama." *The Western Journal of Black Studies* 14.2 (1990): 136-141.

Aston, Elaine. "Male Impersonation in the Music Hall: the Case of Vesta Tilly." *New Theatre Quarterly* 15 (1988): 247-257.

———. *An Introduction to Feminism and Theatre.* New York: Routledge, 1995.

Aston, Elaine, and G. Savona. *Theatre as Sign-System: A Semiotics of Text and Performance.* New York: Routledge, 1991.

Austin, Gayle. *Feminist Theories for Dramatic Criticism.* Ann Arbor: University of Michigan Press, 1990.

Baker, Houston A. *Black Studies, Rap, and the Academy.* Chicago: University of Chicago Press, 1993.

Baker, Jean-Claude. *Josephine: The Hungry Heart.* New York: Random House, 1993.

Baker, Josephine, and Jo Bouillion. *Josephine.* New York: Harper & Row, 1977.

Banes, Sally. *Writing Dancing in the Age of Postmodernism.* Hanover, NH: University Press of New England, 1994.

Barnes, Ruth and Eicher, Joanne B., ed., *Dress and Gender: Making and Meaning.* Oxford: Berg, 1992.

Battle, Effie T., Gertrude Arquene Fisher, and Myra Viola Wilds. *Six Poets of Racial Uplift (African-American Women Writers, 1910-1940).* New York: GK Hall, 1996.

Begho, Felix O. *Black Dance Continuum: Reflections on the Heritage Connection Between African Dance and Afro-American Jazz Dance.* Diss, Ann Arbor: University of Michigan Press, 1990. 8510749.

Benson, Susan P., Stephen Brier, and Roy Rosenzweig, eds. *Presenting The Past: Essays on History and the Public.* Philadelphia: Temple University Press, 1986.

Best, James J. *American Popular Illustration: A Reference Guide.* Westport, CT: Greenwillow Press, 1984.

Black Tradition in American Modern Dance. Durham, NC: American Dance Festival, 1988.

Blair, John. "Blackface Minstrels in Cross-Cultural Perspective." *American Studies International* 28.2 (1990): 52-65.

Blesh, Rudi, and Harriet Janis. *They All Played Ragtime.* New York: Alfred A. Knopf, 1950.

Bogle, Donald. *Toms, Coons, Mulattoes, Mammies, and Bucks.* New York: Continuum, 1973.

Bordman, Gerald Martin. *American Musical Comedy: From Adonis To Dreamgirls.* New York: Oxford University Press, 1982.

Boskin, Joseph. *Sambo: The Rise and Demise of an American Jester.* New York: Oxford University Press, 1986.

Boucicault, Dion. *The Octoroon, or Life in Louisiana. A Play in Five Acts.* North Stratford, NH: Ayer Company, 1977.

Brandon, Harry P. "Harlem Home of the Stage." *The Philadelphia Tribune* (October 3, 1940): 14.

Brown, Buster. Interview with Dianne Walker. Oral History Project. Dance Collection. New York Public Library. Saturday, February 8, 1997, 5:00 P.M.

Brown, Cecelia R. "The Afro-American Contribution to Dance in the United States, 1619-1965." *Negro Heritage* 14.3 (1975): 63-71.

Brown, Elsa Barkley. "What Has Happened Here: The Politics of Difference in Women's History and Feminist Politics." In *We Specialize in the Wholly Impossible,* ed. Darlene Clark Hine, Wilma King, Linda Reed. New York: Carlson, 1995.

Brown, Janet. *Feminist Drama: Definition and Critical Analysis.* Metuchen, NJ: Scarecrow Press, 1979.

————. *Taking Center Stage: Feminism in Contemporary U.S. Drama.* Metuchen, NJ: Scarecrow Press, 1991.

Brown-Guillory, Elizabeth. *Their Place on the Stage: Black Women Playwrights in America.* New York: Greenwood Press, 1988.

Bryant-Jackson, Paul K., and Lois More Overbeck, eds. *Intersecting Boundaries: The Theatre of Adrienne Kennedy.* Minneapolis: University of Minnesota Press, 1992.

Butcher, Margaret Just. *The Negro in American Culture.* New York: Alfred A. Knopf, 1972.

Butler, Judith. *Bodies That Matter.* New York: Routledge, 1993.

————. *Gender Trouble: Feminism and the Subversion of Identity.* London: Routledge, 1990.

————. "Performative Acts and Gender Constitution: An Essay in Phenomenology and Feminist Theory." In *Performing Feminisms: Feminist Critical Theory and Theatre*, ed. Sue-Ellen Case. London: Johns Hopkins University Press, 1990.

Carby, Hazel V. *Reconstructing Womanhood: The Emergence of the Afro-American Woman Novelist*. New York: Oxford University Press, 1987.

Carter, Steven R. *Hansberry's Drama*. New York: Meridian, 1993.

Case, Sue-Ellen, ed. *Feminism and Theatre*. New York: Routledge, 1988.

————. *Performing Feminisms: Feminist Critical Theory and Theatre*. London: Johns Hopkins University Press, 1990.

Cayton, Mary K., Elliott J. Gorn, and Peter W. Williams, eds. *Encyclopedia of American Social History*. New York: Scribner, 1993.

Christian, Barbara. *Black Women Novelists: The Development of a Tradition, 1892-1976*. Westport, CT: Greenwood Press, 1980.

————. *Black Feminist Criticism: Perspectives on Black Women Writers*. New York: Pergamon Press, 1985.

————. "The Race for Theory." *Feminist Studies* 14.1 (Spring 1988): 67-79.

Cixous, Helene. "Aller á la Mer." *Modern Drama* 27.4 (December 1984): 546-548.

Clark, VèVè A. "The Archaeology of Black Theatre." *The Black Scholar* 10.10 (1979): 43-56.

————. "Performing the Memory of Difference in Afro-Caribbean Dance: Katherine Dunham's Choreography, 1938-87." In *History and Memory in African American Culture*, ed. Genevieve Fabre and Robert O'Meally. New York: Oxford University Press, 1994.

Clark, VèVè A., Ruth-Ellen B. Joeres, and Madelon Sprengnether, eds. *Revising the Word and the World: Essays in Feminist Literary Criticism*. Chicago: The University of Chicago Press, 1993.

Clarke, Breena, and Glenda Dickerson. "Re/membering Aunt Jemima: A Menstrual Show." *Women and Performance* 6.1 (1993): 95-130. Reprinted in *Colored Contradictions: An Anthology of Contemporary African-American Plays*, ed. Harry J. Elam and Robert Alexander (New York: Plume, 1996), 141-171.

————. "Re/membering Aunt Jemima: Rescuing the Secret Voice." *Women and Performance* 6.1 (1993): 77-94.

Collins, Patricia Hill. *Black Feminist Thought: Knowledge, Consciousness, and the Politics of Empowerment*. New York: Routledge, 1991.

Cooper, Anna Julia. *A Voice From the South*. New York: Oxford University Press, 1988.

Cowan, Tom, and Jack Maguire. *Timelines of African-American History: 500 Years of Black Achievement*. New York: Roundtable Press, 1994.

Craig, Evelyn Quita. *Black Drama of The Federal Theatre Era: Beyond The Formal Horizons*. Amherst: University of Massachusetts Press, 1980.

Dance Black America: April 21-24, 1983. Brooklyn, NY: Brooklyn Academy of Music, 1983.

Dance Research Journal: Popular Dance in Black America 15.2 (Spring 1983).

Daughtry, Willa. *Sissieretta Jones: A Study of the Negro's Contribution to the Nineteenth-Century American Concert and Theatrical Life.* Diss. Syracuse University. 1968. Ann Arbor: University of Michigan Press, 1968. 68-13,823.

Davis, Angela. *Angela Davis: An Autobiography.* New York: Random House, 1974.

———. *Women, Race and Class.* New York: Vintage Books, 1981.

Davis, Lindsay Elizabeth. *Lifting as They Climb.* Washington, D.C.: National Association of Colored J. W. Women, n.d.

Davis, Tracy C. *Actresses as Working Women: Their Social Identity in Victorian Culture.* New York: Routledge, 1991.

De Lauretis, Teresa. *Alice Doesn't: Feminism, Semiotics, Cinema.* Bloomington: Indiana University Press, 1984.

———. *Technologies of Gender: Essays on Theory, Film, and Fiction.* Bloomington: Indiana University Press, 1987.

Dickerson, Glenda. "The Cult of True Womanhood: Toward a Womanist Attitude in African-American Theatre." In *Performing Feminisms,* ed. Sue-Ellen Case. Baltimore: The Johns Hopkins University Press, 1990.

Dixon, Brenda. "Reports: You've Taken My Blues and Gone: A Seminar on Black Dance in White America." *Dance Research Journal* 16.2 (Fall 1984).

———. "Black Dance and Dancers and the White Public: A Prolegomenon to Problems of Definition." In *American Dance Festival: The Black Tradition in American Modern Dance.* Durham, N.C.: American Dance Festival, 1988.

Dolan, Jill. "The Feminist Spectator as Critic." In *Theater and Dramatic Studies* 52. Ann Arbor: University of Michigan Research Press, 1988.

———. *Presence and Desire.* Ann Arbor: University of Michigan Press, 1993.

———. *The Feminist Spectator as Critic.* Ann Arbor: University of Michigan Press, 1994.

Donkin, Ellen, and Susan Clement, eds. *Upstaging Big Daddy: Directing Theater as if Gender and Race Matter.* Ann Arbor: University of Michigan Press, 1993.

Dyer, Richard. *Only Entertainment.* New York: Routledge, 1992.

Dyson, Michael Eric. *Reflecting Black: African American Cultural Criticism.* Minneapolis: University of Minnesota Press, 1993.

Elam, Harry J., and Robert Alexander, eds. *Colored Contradictions: An Anthology of Contemporary African American Plays.* New York: Plume, 1996.

Ely, Melvin Patrick. *The Adventures of Amos 'n' Andy: A Social History of an American Phenomenon.* New York: Free Press, 1991.

Emery, Lynne Fauley. *Black Dance: From 1619 to Today.* Princeton, NJ: Princeton Book Company, 1988.

Engle, Gary D. *This Grotesque Essence: Plays from the American Minstrel Stage.* Baton Rouge: Louisiana State University Press, 1978.

Erenberg, Lewis A. *Steppin' Out: New York Nightlife and the Transformation of American Culture, 1890-1930.* Westport, CT: Greenwood Press, 1981.

Ethnic Notions. Dir. Marlon Riggs. California Newsreel, 1986.

Fabre, Genevieve. *Drumbeats, Masks, and Metaphor: Contemporary Afro-American Theatre.* Cambridge, MA: Harvard University Press, 1983.

———. "Festive Moments in Antebellum African American Culture." In *The Black Columbiad: Defining Moments in African American Literature and Culture,* ed. Werner Sollors and Maria Diedrich. Cambridge, MA: Harvard University Press, 1994.

———. "African-American Commemorative Celebrations in the Nineteenth Century." In *History and Memory in African-American Culture,* ed. Geneviève Fabre and Robert O'Meally. Oxford University Press, 1994.

Felski, Rita. *Beyond Feminist Aesthetics: Feminist Literature and Social Change.* Cambridge, MA: Harvard University Press, 1989.

Ferguson, Blanche. "Black Skin, Black Mask: The Inconvenient Grace of Bert Williams." *American Visions* 7.3 (June/July 1992): 14.

Ferris, Lesley. *Acting Women: Images of Women in Theatre.* New York: New York University Press, 1989.

———, ed. *Crossing the Stage: Controversies on Cross-Dressing.* New York: Routledge, 1993.

Fletcher, Tom. *100 Years of the Negro in Show Business.* New York: Da Capo Press, 1984.

Foster, Stephen Collins. *Minstrel-Show Songs.* New York: Da Capo Press, 1980.

Fraden, Rena. *Blueprints for a Black Federal Theatre, 1935-1939.* New York: Cambridge University Press, 1994.

Frank, Rusty E. *Tap! The Greatest Tap Dance Stars and Their Stories, 1900-1955.* New York: Da Capo Press, 1994.

Gabriel, John. *Racism, Culture, Markets.* New York: Routledge, 1994.

Gaines, Kevin K. *Uplifting the Race: Black Leadership, Politics, and Culture in the Twentieth Century.* Chapel Hill: University of North Carolina Press, 1996.

Gans, Herbert J. *Popular Culture and High Culture: An Analysis and Evaluation of Taste.* New York: Basic Books, 1975.

Gates, Henry Louis, Jr. *The Signifying Monkey: A Theory of African American Literary Criticism.* New York: Oxford University Press, 1988.

———, ed. *Reading Black, Reading Feminist: A Critical Anthology.* New York: Meridian, 1990.

Gavin, James. *Intimate Nights: The Golden Age of New York Cabaret.* New York: Grove Weidenfeld, 1991.

Gerould, Daniel C. *American Melodrama*. New York: Performing Arts Journal Publications, 1983.

Giddings, Paula. *When and Where I Enter: The Impact of Black Women on Race and Sex in America*. New York: Bantam Books, 1984.

Gilbert, Douglas. *American Vaudeville, Its Life and Times*. New York: Dover Publications, 1963.

Gilroy, Paul. *The Black Atlantic: Modernity and Double Consciousness*. Cambridge, MA: Harvard University Press, 1993.

Ginzburg, Ralph. *100 Years of Lynchings*. Baltimore, MD: Black Classic Press, 1988.

Goines, Margaretta Bobo. "African Retentions in the Dance of the Americas." In *Dance Research Monograph One 1971-1972*. New York: CORD, 1973, 207-229.

Goings, Kenneth W. *Mammy and Uncle Mose: Black Collectibles and American Stereotyping*. Bloomington: Indiana University Press, 1994.

Goss, Wade Tynes Pretlow, and Julinda Lewis-Williams. "A Call for Valid Black Dance Criticism." In *Dance Research Collage*. New York: CORD, 1979, 77-80.

Gottschild, Brenda Dixon. *Digging the Africanist Presence in American Performance: Dance and Other Contexts*. Westport, CT: Greenwood Press, 1996.

Green, Abel. *Show Biz, From Vaude to Video*. New York: Holt, 1951.

Grimsted, David. *Melodrama Unveiled; American Theater and Culture, 1800-1850*. Chicago: University of Chicago Press, 1968.

Guild, Leo. *Josephine Baker*. Los Angeles, CA: Holloway House, 1976.

Hamalian, Leo, and Hatch James V. *The Roots of African American Drama: An Anthology of Early Plays, 1858-1938*. Detroit: Wayne State University Press, 1991

Haney, Lynn. *Naked at the Feast: A Biography of Josephine Baker*. New York: Dodd, Mead, 1981.

Hansberry, Lorraine. "The Negro Writer and His Roots: Toward a New Romanticism." *The Black Scholar*, 12.2 (1981): 2-12.

Harlon, Louis H., ed. *The Booker T. Washington Papers*, Vol. 3. Chicago: University of Illinois Press, 1974.

Harris, Clarissa Myrick. *Mirror of the Movement: The History of the Free Southern Theater as a Microcosm of the Civil Rights and Black Power Movements, 1963-1978*. Diss., Emory University, 1988. Ann Arbor: University of Michigan Press, 1989. 8827899.

Harris, Middleton, Morris Levitt, Roger Furman, Ernest Smith. *The Black Book*. New York: Random House, 1974.

Harrison, Daphne Duval. *Black Pearls: Blues Queens of the 1920s*. New Brunswick, NJ: Rutgers University Press, 1993.

Harrison, Paul Carter. *The Drama of Nommo*. New York: Grove Press, 1972.

———. *Totem Voices: Plays from The Black World Repertory*. New York: Grove Press, 1989.

Hart, Lynda. *Fatal Women: Lesbian Sexuality and the Mark of Aggression*. Princeton, NJ: Princeton University Press, 1994.

Hart, Lynda, and Peggy Phelan, eds. *Acting Out: Feminist Performances*. Ann Arbor: University of Michigan Press, 1993.

Haskins, James. *The Cotton Club*. New York: Hippocrene Books, 1977.

———. *Black Theater in America*. New York: Crowell, 1982.

———. *Black Dance in America: A History Through Its People*. New York: T. Y. Crowell, 1990.

Hatch, James V., and Leo Hamalian, eds. *Black Image on the American Stage; A Bibliography of Plays and Musicals, 1770-1970*. New York: DBS Publications, 1970.

———. *Black Theater U.S.A.: Forty-Five Plays by Black Americans 1847-1974*. New York: The Free Press, 1974.

———. *The Roots of African American Drama: An Anthology of Early Plays, 1858-1938*. Detroit: Wayne State University Press, 1991.

Hay, Samuel A. *African American Theatre: A Historical and Critical Analysis*. New York: Cambridge University Press, 1994.

Hayes, Donald. *An Analysis of Dramatic Themes Used by Selected Black-American Playwrights from 1950-1976: With a Backgrounder, The State of the Art of the Contemporary Black Theater and Black Playwriting*. Diss. Wayne State University, 1984. Ann Arbor: University of Michigan Press, 1992. 8504881.

Hazzard-Gordon, Katrina. *Jookin': The Rise of Social Dance Formations in African American Culture*. Philadelphia: Temple University Press, 1990.

Higginbotham, Evelyn Brooks. *Righteous Discontent: The Women's Movement in the Black Baptist Church, 1880-1920*. Cambridge, MA: Harvard University Press, 1993.

———. "African-American Women's History and the Metalanguage of Race," in *We Specialize in the Wholly Impossible: A Reader in Black Women's History*, ed. Darlene Clark Hine et al. Brooklyn: Carlson, 1995, 487-503.

Hill, Constance. "Katherine Dunham's Southland: Protest in the Face of Repression." *Dance Research Journal* (Fall 1994): 1-10.

Hill, Errol, ed. *The Theatre of Black Americans: A Collection of Critical Essays*. New York: Applause Theatre Book Publishers, 1987.

Hine, Darlene Clark, Wilma King, Linda Reed, eds. *We Specialize in the Wholly Impossible: A Reader in Black Women's History*. New York: Carlson, 1995.

Hinton, Robert. "Black Dance in American History," *American Dance Festival: The Black Tradition in American Modern Dance*. Durham, NC: American Dance Festival, 1988.

Hoffmann, Frank W. *American Popular Culture: A Guide to the Reference Literature*. Englewood, CO: Libraries Unlimited, 1995.

hooks, bell. *Talking Back: Thinking Feminist, Thinking Black*. Boston: South End Press, 1989.

————. *Yearning: Race, Gender, and Cultural Politics*. Boston: South End Press, 1990.

————. *Black Looks: Race and Representation*. Boston: South End Press, 1992.

Hughes, Langston. "Black Influences in the American Theater." In *The Black American Reference Book*. Englewood Cliffs, NJ: Prentice Hall, 1976.

Hughes, Langston, and Milton Meltzer. *Black Magic: A Pictorial History Of The African American in The Performing Arts*. New York: Da Capo Press, 1990.

Inge, Thomas M. *Handbook of American Popular Culture*. New York: Greenwood Press, 1989.

Irigaray, Luce. "This Sex Which Is Not One." Trans. C. Reeder, in E. Marks and I. de Courtivron, eds. *New French Feminisms*. Brighton: Harvester Press, 1981.

————. *je, tu, nous: Toward a Culture of Difference*. Trans. A. Martin. New York: Routledge, 1993.

James, Stanlie M., and Abena P. A. Busia. *Theorizing Black Feminisms: The Visionary Pragmatism of Black Women*. New York: Routledge, 1993.

Jewell, K. Sue. *From Mammy to Miss America and Beyond: Cultural Images and the Shaping of U.S. Policy*. New York: Routledge, 1993.

Johns, Robert L. "The Whitman Sisters." In *Notable Black Women, Book II*, ed. Jessie Carney Smith. New York: Gale Research, 1996.

Johnson, Helen Armstead. "Blacks in Vaudeville: Broadway and Beyond." In *American Popular Entertainment: Papers and Proceedings of the Conference on the History of American Popular Entertainment*, ed. Myron Matlaw. Westport, CT: Greenwood Press, 1979.

Johnson, James Weldon. *The Book of American Negro Spirituals*. New York: Viking Press, 1925.

————. *Black Manhattan*. New York: A. A. Knopf, 1930.

Johnson, Theodore Wallace. *Black Images in American Popular Song, 1840-1910*. Diss., Northwestern University., 1975.

Jones, Jacqueline. *Labor of Love, Labor of Sorrow: Black Women, Work, and the Family From Slavery to the Present*. New York: Basic Books, 1985

Keyssar, Helene. *The Curtain and the Veil: Strategies in Black Drama*. New York: B. Franklin, 1981.

King, Woodie. *Black Theatre, Present Condition*. New York: National Black Theatre Touring Circuit, 1981.

King, Woodie, and Ron Milner, eds. *Black Drama Anthology*. New York: Penguin Books, 1971.

Krasner, David. *Resistance, Parody, and Double Consciousness in African American Theatre, 1895-1910*. New York: St. Martin's Press, 1997.

Laforse, Martin W. *Popular Culture and American Life: Selected Topics in the Study of American Popular Culture*. Chicago: Nelson-Hall, 1981.

Landrum, Larry N. *American Popular Culture: A Guide to Information Sources.* Detroit, MI: Gale Research, 1982.

Laughlin, Karen and Catherine Schuler, eds. *Theatre and Feminist Aesthetics.* Madison, NJ: Fairleigh Dickinson University Press, 1995.

Laurie, Joseph. *Vaudeville: From the Honky-Tonks to the Palace.* New York: Holt, 1953.

Leonard, William T. *Masquerade in Black.* Metuchen, NJ: Scarecrow Press, 1986.

Lerner, Gerda. *Black Women in America: A Documentary History.* New York: Pantheon Books, 1972.

———. *The Majority Finds Its Past: Placing Women in History.* New York: Oxford University Press, 1979.

Levine, Lawrence W. *Black Culture and Black Consciousness: Afro-American Folk Thought from Slavery to Freedom.* New York: Oxford University Press, 1977.

———. *Highbrow/Lowbrow: The Emergence of Cultural Hierarchy in America.* Cambridge, MA: Harvard University Press, 1988.

Levinson, Andre. "The Negro Dance Under European Eyes." *Theatre Arts* (April 1927): 282-293.

Lewis, David Levering. *When Harlem Was in Vogue.* New York: Oxford University Press, 1981.

Lewis-Furguson, Julinda, ed. *Black Choreographers Moving: Papers, Panels, and Interviews from the 1989 National Dance Festival.* Berkeley, CA: Expansion Arts Service, 1991.

Long, Richard A. *Black Dance: The Black Tradition in American Modern Dance.* New York: Rizzoli, 1989.

Lorde, Audre. *Sister Outsider.* Freedom, CA: The Crossing Press, 1984.

Lott, Eric. *Love and Theft: Blackface Minstrelsy and the American Working Class.* New York: Oxford University Press, 1993.

Lucas, Ernestine Garrett. *Wider Windows to the Past: African American History from a Family Perspective.* Decorah, Iowa: Anundsen, 1995.

Mahone, Sydné, ed. *Moon Marked and Touched By Sun: Plays By African American Women.* New York: Theatre Communications Group, 1994.

Malone, Jacqui. *Steppin' on the Blues: The Visible Rhythms of African American Dance.* Chicago: University of Illinois Press, 1996.

Malpede, Karen, ed. *Women in Theatre: Compassion and Hope.* New York: Drama Book, 1983.

Marsh, J. B. T. *The Story of the Jubilee Singers; with Their Songs.* New York: Negro Universities Press, 1969.

Marston, William Moulton. *F. F. Proctor, Vaudeville Pioneer.* New York: R. R. Smith, 1943.

Martin, Elmer P., and Joanne Mitchell, *The Black Extended Family.* Chicago: University of Chicago Press, 1978.

Mason, Herman. *African-American Entertainment in Atlanta*. Atlanta: Arcadia Tempus
     Publishing Group, 1998.
Mason, Jeffrey D. *Melodrama and the Myth of America*. Bloomington: Indiana University
     Press, 1993.
Matlaw, Myron, ed. *American Popular Entertainment: Papers and Proceedings of the Conference
     on the History of American Popular Entertainment*. Westport, CT: Greenwood
     Press, 1979.
McAllister, Marvin Edward. *"White People Do Not Know How to Behave at Entertainments
     Designed For Ladies and Gentlemen of Color": A History of New York's African Grove/
     African Theatre*. Diss, Northwestern University., 1997. 9731301.
McConachie, Bruce A. *Melodramatic Formations: American Theatre and Society, 1820-1870*.
     Iowa City: University of Iowa Press, 1992.
McConachie, Bruce A. and Thomas Postlewait, eds. *Interpreting the Theatrical Past: Essays
     in the Historiography of Performance*. Iowa City: University of Iowa Press, 1991.
McLean, Albert F. *American Vaudeville as Ritual*. Lexington: University of Kentucky
     Press, 1965.
McNamara, Brooks, ed. *American Popular Entertainments: Jokes, Monologues, Bits, and
     Sketches*. New York City: Performing Arts Journal Publications, 1983.
Melosh, Barbara. *Engendering Culture: Manhood and Womanhood in New Deal Public Art and
     Theater*. Washington, D.C.: Smithsonian Institution Press, 1991.
Meyer, Moe, ed. *The Politics and Poetics of Camp*. New York: Routledge, 1994.
Minsky, Morton. *Burlesque*. New York: Arbor House, 1986.
Minstrel-Show Songs. New York: Da Capo Press, 1980.
Mitchell, Loften. *Voices of the Black Theatre*. Clifton, NJ: J. T. White, 1975.
Mollete, Carlton, and Barbara Mollete. *Black Theatre: Premise and Presentation*. Bristol,
     IN: Wyndham Hall Press, 1986.
Morrison, Toni. "The Site of Memory." *Out There: Marginalization and Contemporary
     Cultures*, ed. Russell Ferguson and Martha Gever. Cambridge: MIT Press,
     1990.
Motz, Marilyn E. ed. *Eye On The Future: Popular Culture Scholarship into the Twenty-First
     Century in Honor of Ray B. Browne*. Bowling Green, OH: Bowling Green State
     University Popular Press, 1994.
Moss, Alfred A. *The American Negro Academy: Voice of the Talented Tenth*. Baton Rouge:
     Louisiana State University Press, 1981.
Mukerji, Chandra, and Michael Schudson, eds. *Rethinking Popular Culture: Contemporary
     Perspectives in Cultural Studies*. Berkeley: University of California Press, 1991.
Mulvey, Laura. "Visual Pleasure and Narrative Cinema," *Screen* 16.3 (1975): 6-18.
Muse, Clarence, and David Arlen. *Way Down South*. Hollywood, CA: David Graham
     Fischer, 1932.

Nasaw, David. *Going Out: The Rise and Fall of Public Amusements.* New York: Basic Books, 1993.

Natelle, Elizabeth J. *Feminist Theatre: A Study in Persuasion.* Metuchen, NJ: Scarecrow Press, 1985.

Nathan, Hans. *Dan Emmett and the Rise of Early Negro Minstrelsy.* Norman: University of Oklahoma Press, 1962.

Neal, Larry. "Toward a Relevant Black Theatre." *Black Theatre* 4 (1969): 14-15.

Neverdon-Morton, Cynthia. *Afro-American Women of the South and the Advancement of the Race, 1895-1925.* Knoxville: University of Tennessee Press, 1989.

New Minstrel and Black Face Joke Book by Leading Footlight Favorites. Baltimore: Ottenheimer, 1907.

Ogunyemi, Chikwenye Okonjo. "Womanism: The Dynamics of the Contemporary Black Female Novel in English." In *Revising the Word and the World,* ed. VéVé Clark, et al. Chicago: University of Chicago Press, 1993.

Olaniyan, Tejumola. *The Poetics and Politics of "Othering": Contemporary African, African American, and Caribbean Drama and the Invention of Cultural Identities.* Diss., Cornell University, 1991. Ann Arbor: University of Michigan Press, 1992. 9203968.

Omi, Michael, and Howard Winant. *Racial Formation in the United States: From 1960s to the 1990s.* New York: Routledge, 1994.

Osumare, Halifu. "An Aesthetic of the Cool Revisited: The Ancestral Dance Link in the African Diaspora." *UCLA Journal of Dance Ethnology* 17 (1993): 1-16.

Parker, Gail. *The Oven Birds: American Woman on Womanhood, 1820-1920.* Garden City, NY: Anchor Books, 1972.

Pascal, Julia. "The Ghetto of Ethnic Dance." *Ballet International* 14.3-4 (March/April 1991).

Paskman, Dailey. *"Gentlemen Be Seated!": A Parade of the American Minstrels.* New York: C. N. Potter, 1976.

Perkins, Linda. "Black Women and the Philosophy of 'Race Uplift' Prior to Emancipation." Cambridge, MA: Mary Ingraham Bunting Institute, Radcliffe College, 1980.

———. "Black Feminism and 'Race Uplift,' 1890-1900." Institute for Independent Study, Radcliffe College, 1981.

Perpener, John O. *The Seminal Years of Black Concert Dance.* Diss., New York University, 1992. Ann Arbor: University of Michigan Press, 1992. 9222911.

Peterson, Bernard L., Jr. *The African American Theatre Directory, 1816-1960: A Comprehensive Guide to Early Black Theatre Organizations, Companies, Theatres, and Performing Groups.* Westport, CT: Greenwood Press, 1997.

———. *A Century of Musicals in Black and White.* Westport, CT: Greenwood Press, 1993.

Poggi, Jack. *Theater in America: The Impact of Economic Forces 1870-1967.* Ithaca, NY: Cornell University Press, 1968.

Porter, Michael Leroy. *Black Atlanta: An Interdisciplinary Study of Blacks of the East Side of Atlanta, 1890-1930.* Dissertation, Emory University, 1974.

Pryse, Marjorie, and Hortense J. Spillers, eds. *Conjuring: Black Women, Fiction and Literary Tradition.* Bloomington: Indiana University Press, 1985.

Reed, Bill. *"Hot From Harlem": Profiles in Classic African-American Entertainment.* Los Angeles: Cellar Door Books, 1998.

Reed, Leonard. Interview with Fred Stickler. Oral History Project. Dance Collection. New York Public Library, 1997.

Reinelt, Janelle G. and Joseph R. Roach, eds. *Critical Theory and Performance.* Ann Arbor: University of Michigan Press, 1992.

Rich, Adrienne. "Notes Toward a Politics of Location." In *Women, Feminist Identity, and Society in the 1980s.* Philadelphia: Benjamins, 1985.

Richards, Sandra L. "Bert Williams: The Man and The Mask." *Mime, Mask & Marionette* 1.1 (Spring 1978): 6-25.

————. "Writing the Absent Potential: Drama, Performance, and the Canon of African-American Literature." In *Performativity and Performance,* ed. Andrew Parker and Eve Kosofsky Sedgwick. New York: Routledge, 1995.

Riis, Thomas L. *Just Before Jazz: Black Musical Theatre in New York, 1890 to 1915.* Washington, D.C.: Smithsonian Institution Press, 1994.

Rose, Phyllis. *Jazz Cleopatra: Josephine Baker in Her Time.* New York: Doubleday, 1989.

Rose, Tricia. *Black Noise: Rap Music and Black Culture In Contemporary America.* Hanover, NH: Wesleyan University Press, University Press of New England, 1994.

Rowland, Mabel. *Bert Williams, Son of Laughter.* New York City: The English Crafters, 1923.

Sacks, Howard L., and Judith Rose Sacks. *Way Up North in Dixie: A Black Family's Claim to the Confederate Anthem.* Washington: Smithsonian Institution Press, 1996.

Sampson, Henry T. *Blacks in Blackface: A Source Book on Early Black Musical Shows.* Metuchen, NJ: Scarecrow Press, 1980.

————. *The Ghost Walks: A Chronological History of Blacks in Show Business, 1865-1910.* Metuchen, NJ: Scarecrow Press, 1988.

Samuels, Charles. *Once Upon a Stage: The Merry World of Vaudeville.* New York: Dodd, Mead, 1974.

Sanders, Leslie Catherine. *The Development of Black Theater in America: From Shadows to Selves.* Baton Rouge: Louisiana State University Press, 1988.

Senelick, Laurence, ed. *Gender in Performance: The Presentation of Difference in the Performing Arts.* Hanover, NH: University Press of New England, 1992.

Shange, Ntozake. "Unrecovered Losses/Black Theatre Traditions," *The Black Scholar* 10.10 (1979): 7-9.

Shaw, Harry B., ed. *Perspectives of Black Popular Culture*. Bowling Green, OH: Bowling Green State University Popular Press, 1990.

Sherman, Joan R. "Albery Allson Whitman: Poet of Beauty and Manliness." *CLA Journal* 1: November (1957): 126-143.

———. *Invisible Poets: Afro-Americans of the Nineteenth Century*. University of Illinois Press: Chicago, 1974.

———. *African American Poetry of the Nineteenth Century*. University of Illinois Press: Chicago, 1992.

Shilling, Chris. *The Body and Social Theory*. London: Sage Publications, 1993.

Shimkin, Demitri B., Edith M. Shimkin, and Dennis A. Frate, eds. *The Extended Family in Black Societies*. Chicago: Aldine, 1978.

Showalter, Elaine, ed. *The New Feminist Criticism: Essays on Women, Literature and Theory*. New York: Panthcon Books, 1985.

Slide, Anthony, ed. *The Vaudevillians: A Dictionary Of Vaudeville Performers*. Westport, CT: Arlington House, 1981.

———. *Selected Vaudeville Criticism*. Metuchen, NJ: Scarecrow Press, 1988.

———. *The Encyclopedia of Vaudeville*. Westport, CT: Greenwood Press, 1994.

Smith, Bill. *The Vaudevillians*. New York: Macmillan, 1976.

Smith, Eric Ledell. *Bert Williams: A Biography of the Pioneer Black Comedian*. Jefferson, NC: McFarland, 1992.

Snyder, Robert W. *The Voice of the City: Vaudeville and Popular Culture in New York*. New York: Oxford University Press, 1989.

Sobel, Bernard. *Burleycue; An Underground History of Burlesque Days*. New York: Farrar & Rinehart, 1931.

———. *A Pictorial History of Burlesque*. New York: Putnam, 1956.

———. *A Pictorial History of Vaudeville*. New York: Citadel Press, 1961.

Southern, Eileen. *The Greenwood Encyclopedia of Black Music*. London: Greenwood Press, 1982.

Spillers, Hortense J. "Mama's Baby, Papa's Maybe: An American Grammar Book." *diacritics* (Summer 1987): 65-81.

Spitzer, Marian. *The Palace*. New York: Atheneum, 1969.

Spivak, Gayatri Chakravorty. *In Other Worlds: Essays in Cultural Politics*. New York: Routledge, 1988.

Staples, Robert. "The Myth of Black Macho: A Response to Angry Black Feminists." *The Black Scholar* 10.10 (1979): 24-33.

Stearns, Marshall, and Jean Stearns. *Jazz Dance: The Story of American Vernacular Dance*. New York: Da Capo Press, 1994.

Stein, Charles W. *American Vaudeville as Seen by Its Contemporaries*. New York: Knopf, 1984.

Stephens, Judith L. "Gender Ideology and Dramatic Convention in Progressive Era Plays, 1890-1920." *Performing Feminisms: Feminist Critical Theory and Theatre*, ed. Sue-Ellen Case. Baltimore: Johns Hopkins University Press, 1990.

Stewart, Maria. "Productions of Mrs. Maria W. Stewart." In *Daughters of Africa: An International Anthology of Words and Writings by Women of African Descent from the Ancient Egyptian to the Present*, ed. Margaret Busby. New York: Ballantine Books, 1992.

Storey, John. *An Introductory Guide to Cultural Theory and Popular Culture*. Athens: University of Georgia Press, 1993.

Stuckley, Sterling. *Slave Culture: Nationalist Theory and the Foundation of Black America*. New York: Oxford University Press, 1987.

———. "The Skies of Consciousness: African Dance at Pinkster in New York, 1750-1840." *Going Through the Storm: The Influence of African American Art in History*. New York: Oxford University Press, 1994.

Tanner, Jo A. *Dusky Maidens: The Odyssey of the Early Black Dramatic Actress*. Westport, CT: Greenwood Press, 1992.

Terborg-Penn, Rosalyn, "Discontented Black Feminist." In *We Specialize in the Wholly Impossible: A Reader in Black Women's History*, ed. Darlene Clark Hine et al. Brooklyn: Carlson, 1995.

Thorpe, Edward. *Black Dance*. Woodstock, NY: The Overlook Press, 1990.

Toll, Robert C. *Blacking Up: The Minstrel Show in Nineteenth Century America*. New York: Oxford University Press, 1974.

———. *On With the Show!: The First Century of Show Business in America*. New York: Oxford University Press, 1976.

———. "Show Biz in Blackface: The Evolution of the Minstrel Show as a Theatrical Form." *American Popular Entertainment*. Westport, CT: Greenwood Press, 1977.

Traylor, Eleanor. "Two Afro-American Contributions to Dramatic Form." In *The Theatre of Black Americans: A Collection of Critical Essays*, ed. Errol Hill. New York: Applause Theatre Book Publishers, 1987.

Turner, Darwin T., ed. *Black Drama in America*. Washington, D.C.: Howard University Press. 1994.

Turner, Patricia A. *Ceramic Uncles & Celluloid Mammies: Black Images and Their Influence on Culture*. New York: Anchor Books, 1994.

Twelfth Census of the United States. Schedule No. 1—Population. Fulton County, Atlanta, Georgia. June 16, 1900.

Van Deburg, William L. *Slavery & Race in American Popular Culture*. Madison: University of Wisconsin Press, 1984.

Vaz, Kim Marie, ed. *Black Women in America*. Thousand Oaks, CA: Sage Publications, 1995.

Walker, Alice. *In Search of Our Mother's Gardens: Womanist Prose.* New York: Harcourt, Brace and Company, 1983.

———. "Giving the Party: Aunt Jemima, Mammy and the Goddess Within." *Ms.* 4. 6 (1994): 22-25.

Wallace, Michele. *Invisibility Blues: From Pop to Theory.* New York: Verso, 1990.

———. *Black Popular Culture.* ed. Gina Dent. Seattle, WA: Bay Press, 1992.

Welter, Barbara. *Dimity Convictions: The American Woman in the Nineteenth Century.* Athens: Ohio University Press, 1976.

Wertheim, Arthur F., ed. *American Popular Culture: A Historical Bibliography.* Santa Barbara, CA: ABC-Clio Information Services, 1984.

White, David M., and John Pendleton, eds. *Popular Culture: Mirror of American Life.* Del Mar, CA: Publisher's, 1977.

Wilkerson, Margaret B. "Redefining Black Theatre." *The Black Scholar* 10.10 (1979): 32-42.

Williams, Mance. *Black Theatre in the 1960s and 1970s: A Historical-Critical Analysis of the Movement.* Westport, CT: Greenwood Press, 1985.

Wilmeth, Don B. *American and English Popular Entertainment: A Guide to Information Sources.* Detroit: Gale Research, 1980.

Wittke, Carl Frederick. *Tambo And Bones; A History of The American Minstrel Stage.* New York: Greenwood Press, 1968.

Woll, Allen. *Black Musical Theatre: From Coontown to Dreamgirls.* New York: Da Capo Press, 1989.

Woodson, Carter G. *The Mis-Education of the Negro.* London: African World Press, 1990.

X, Marvin. "Manifesto: The Black Educational Theatre of San Francisco." *Black Theatre* 6 (1972): 30-35.

Young, Jackie. *Black Collectibles: Mammy and Her Friends.* West Chester, PA: Schiffer, 1988.

Zeidman, Irving. *The American Burlesque Show.* New York: Hawthorn Books, 1967.

Index

(italics indicate photo)